Cambridge

Elements in Corporate Governance
edited by
Thomas Clarke
UTS Business School, University of Technology Sydney

INVESTING IN INNOVATION

Confronting Predatory Value Extraction in the US Corporation

William Lazonick
The Academic-Industry Research Network

CAMBRIDGE
UNIVERSITY PRESS

Shaftesbury Road, Cambridge CB2 8EA, United Kingdom

One Liberty Plaza, 20th Floor, New York, NY 10006, USA

477 Williamstown Road, Port Melbourne, VIC 3207, Australia

314–321, 3rd Floor, Plot 3, Splendor Forum, Jasola District Centre, New Delhi – 110025, India

103 Penang Road, #05–06/07, Visioncrest Commercial, Singapore 238467

Cambridge University Press is part of Cambridge University Press & Assessment, a department of the University of Cambridge.

We share the University's mission to contribute to society through the pursuit of education, learning and research at the highest international levels of excellence.

www.cambridge.org
Information on this title: www.cambridge.org/9781009410731

DOI: 10.1017/9781009410700

First published 2023

A catalogue record for this publication is available from the British Library.

ISBN 978-1-009-41073-1 Paperback
ISSN 2515-7175 (online)
ISSN 2515-7167 (print)

Investing in Innovation

Confronting Predatory Value Extraction in the US Corporation

Elements in Corporate Governance

DOI: 10.1017/9781009410700
First published online: May 2023

William Lazonick
The Academic-Industry Research Network

Author for correspondence: William Lazonick, william.lazonick@gmail.com

Abstract: Business corporations interact with household units and government agencies to make investments in productive capabilities required to generate innovative goods and services. When they work harmoniously, these three types of organizations constitute "the investment triad." The Biden administration's Build Back Better agenda to restore sustainable prosperity in the United States has focused on investment in productive capabilities by government agencies and household units. Largely absent from the Biden agenda have been policy initiatives to ensure that, given government and household investment in productive capabilities, the governance of major US business corporations supports investment in innovation. This Element explains how corporate financialization, manifested by predatory value extraction in the name of "maximizing shareholder value," undermines investment in innovation in the United States. It concludes by outlining a policy framework, beginning with a ban on stock buybacks, that confronts predatory value extraction and puts in place social institutions that support sustainable prosperity.

Keywords: innovation, financialization, corporate governance, value creation, value extraction

ISBNs: 9781009410731 (PB), 9781009410700 (OC)
ISSNs: 2515-7175 (online), 2515-7167 (print)

Contents

1 Productive Capabilities and Sustainable Prosperity

"Sustainable prosperity" denotes an economy that generates stable and equitable growth for a large and growing middle class. From the 1940s into the 1970s, the United States appeared to be on a trajectory of sustainable prosperity, especially for white-male members of the US labor force.[1] Since the 1980s, however, an increasing proportion of the US labor force has experienced unstable employment and inequitable income, while growing numbers of the business corporations upon which they rely for employment have experienced anemic productivity growth.[2]

Stable and equitable growth requires innovative enterprise. The essence of innovative enterprise is investment in productive capabilities that can generate higher-quality, lower-cost goods and services than those previously available. The innovative enterprise tends to be a business corporation – a unit of strategic control that, by selling products, must make profits over time to survive. In a modern society, however, business corporations are not alone in making investments in the productive capabilities required to generate innovative goods and services. Household units and government agencies also make investments in productive capabilities upon which business corporations rely for their own investment activities. When they work in a harmonious fashion, these three types of organizations – household units, government agencies, and business corporations – constitute "the investment triad."[3]

---

[1] William Lazonick, Philip Moss, Hal Salzman, and Öner Tulum "Skill Development and Sustainable Prosperity: Collective and Cumulative Careers versus Skill-Biased Technical Change," Institute for New Economic Thinking Working Group on the Political Economy of Distribution Working Paper No. 7, December 2014, https://www.ineteconomics.org/research/research-papers/skill-development-and-sustainable-prosperity-cumulative-and-collective-careers-versus-skill-biased-technical-change; William Lazonick, "Labor in the Twenty-First Century: The Top 0.1% and the Disappearing Middle Class," in Christian E. Weller, ed., *Inequality, Uncertainty, and Opportunity: The Varied and Growing Role of Finance in Labor Relations*, Cornell University Press, 2015: 143–192; William Lazonick, Philip Moss, and Joshua Weitz, "How the Disappearance of Unionized Jobs Obliterated an Emergent Black Middle Class," Institute for New Economic Thinking Working Paper No. 125, June 15, 2020, https://www.ineteconomics.org/research/research-papers/how-the-disappearance-of-unionized-jobs-obliterated-an-emergent-black-middle-class.

[2] William Lazonick, "The New Normal is 'Maximizing Shareholder Value': Predatory Value Extraction, Slowing Productivity, and the Vanishing Middle Class," *International Journal of Political Economy*, 46, 4, 2017: 217–226; William Lazonick, and Jang-Sup Shin, *Predatory Value Extraction: How the Looting of the Business Corporation Became the US Norm and How Sustainable Prosperity Can Be Restored*, Oxford University Press, 2020, Ch. 1; William Lazonick, Philip Moss, and Joshua Weitz, "'Build Back Better' Needs an Agenda for Upward Mobility," *Institute for New Economic Thinking*, January 25, 2021, https://www.ineteconomics.org/perspectives/blog/build-back-better-needs-an-agenda-for-upward-mobility.

[3] William Lazonick "The Investment Triad and Sustainable Prosperity," in Peter Creticos, Larry Bennett, Laura Owen, Costas Spirou, and Maxine Morphis-Riesbeck, eds., *The Many Futures of Work: Rethinking Expectations and Breaking Molds*, Temple University Press, 2021: 120–151.

The Biden administration's Build Back Better agenda to restore sustainable prosperity in the United States has focused on investment in productive capabilities by two of the three types of organizations in the triad: *government agencies*, implementing the Infrastructure Investment and Jobs Act of 2021, supplemented by the CHIPS and Science Act of 2022 as well as the Inflation Reduction Act of 2022,[4] and *household units,* envisioned by the American Families Act, which, blocked in the Senate, fell by the wayside during the first two years of Joe Biden's presidency.[5] Largely absent, from the Build Back Better agenda have been policy initiatives to ensure that, given government and household investment in productive capabilities, the executives who control resource allocation in major US *business corporations* have both the abilities and incentives to invest in innovation.

This lacuna is problematic because many of the largest industrial corporations in the United States place a far higher priority on distributing cash to shareholders in the form of dividends and share repurchases for the sake of higher stock yields than on investing in the productive capabilities of their workforces for the sake of innovation. Based on analyses of the "financialization" of major US business corporations, I argue that, unless the Biden administration includes an effective policy agenda to ensure corporate investment in innovation, its program for attaining stable and equitable growth will fail.

What does the investment triad do?

- *Household units* invest in the education of the young with a view toward providing them with the knowledge and aptitudes that they will need to function as productive adults. Later, these younger adults may use the income from productive employment to raise families of their own. Critical determinants of household investments in productive capabilities are the employment incomes earned by parents, their provision of household services, the quality of education available to the young, and the number of years over which they receive their education. Household units also invest in critical

---

[4] US House of Representatives, "H.R. 3684 – Infrastructure Investment and Jobs Act," 117th Congress (2021–2022), *Congress.gov*, November 15, 2021, https://www.congress.gov/bill/117th-congress/house-bill/3684; US House of Representatives, "H.R. 4346 – Chips and Sciences Act," 117th Congress (2021–2022), *Congress.gov*, August 9, 2022, www.congress.gov/bill/117th-congress/house-bill/4346. (Note: Technically, the Chips-Plus package, or what is often called the CHIPS and Science Act, combines "CHIPS Act"; "Research and Development, Competition and Innovation Act"; and "Supreme Court Security Funding Act"); US House of Representatives, "H.R. 5376 – Inflation Reduction Act of 2022," 117th Congress (2021–2022), *Congress.gov*, August 16, 2022, www.congress.gov/bill/117th-congress/house-bill/5376/text.

[5] US House of Representatives, "H.R. 928 – American Family Act of 2021," 117th Congress (2021–2022), *Congress.gov*, February 8, 2021, https://www.congress.gov/bill/117th-congress/house-bill/928.

physical infrastructure in the form of homes. A productive society requires these investments from the *supportive family.*

- *Government agencies* support investments in productive capabilities made by household units by providing schooling that households could not afford on their own. A well-financed primary, secondary, and tertiary education system is a necessary condition for society to embark on a path of sustained development that can enable most of the population to attain higher living standards.[6] By supporting basic and applied research, government agencies can also be charged with investing in the creation of new scientific and engineering knowledge that would otherwise not come into existence. As a critical component of investment in productive capabilities, government agencies provide services for public and personal health. In addition, government agencies invest in physical infrastructure such as transportation systems, communication systems, energy systems, and water and waste systems. Government investments in productive resources, both human capabilities and physical infrastructure, manifest the presence of the *developmental state.*

- *Business corporations* make use of the capabilities and infrastructure provided by government and household investments as foundations for further in-house investment in human resources in combination with expenditure on plant and equipment. Their purpose is the generation of goods and services to be sold in product markets at prices that exceed costs. In high-tech fields, business corporations may need to make specialized in-house investments in capabilities to absorb the advanced knowledge resulting from investments by government agencies. In many cases, government agencies make strategic investments in knowledge creation through business corporations in the form of research contracts, procurement contracts, and financial subsidies. It is typically through on-the-job experience in business corporations and government agencies that individuals build on their formal educations and accumulate the productive capabilities that enable them to contribute to the innovation process. The development and utilization of these productive capabilities are the essence of *innovative enterprise.*

The fundamental weakness of the neoclassical theory of the market economy, which dominates the conventional view of how an advanced economy should function to achieve superior economic performance, is that it lacks a theory of

---

[6] William Lazonick, *Sustainable Prosperity in the New Economy? Business Organization and High-Tech Employment in the United States*, Upjohn Institute for Employment Research, 2009, Ch. 5, https://research.upjohn.org/up_press/13/.

innovative enterprise.[7] Indeed, the conventional "theory of the firm" that posits "perfect competition" as the ideal, even if unattainable, foundation for superior economic performance is based on the obviously absurd argument that the more unproductive the firm, the more efficient the allocation of the economy's resources.[8] This view of the world promotes government policies that seek to make "the market" omnipotent and "the firm" impotent in the resource-allocation process.[9]

If a society wants to attain higher living standards, it needs highly productive, and powerful, business corporations that transform technologies and access markets to generate higher-quality, lower-cost products – the definition of innovative enterprise. The most successful of these corporations inevitably gain substantial power over the allocation of the economy's resources and the operation of its markets. If left unchecked, these powerful corporations can fall prey to "predatory value extraction," as certain parties, including senior executives and activist shareholders who extract far more value from the corporations than they contribute to value creation by the corporation, exercise strategic control over the allocation of the corporation's vast resources.[10] For the sake of attaining stable and equitable growth, these large and powerful corporations must be governed for the common good. The centrality of the investment triad to innovative enterprise provides an economic as well as moral basis for the implementation of institutions of corporate governance for achieving these social objectives.[11]

With appropriate governance institutions in place, the investment triad enables innovative enterprise to function as a foundation for sustainable prosperity. Stable and equitable growth occurs when the investment strategies of households, governments, and businesses interact as supportive families, developmental states, and innovative enterprises. Households and governments interact through investments in education. Governments and businesses interact in the development of the high-tech knowledge base. Businesses and households interact through the employment relationship.

---

[7] William Lazonick, *Business Organization and the Myth of the Market Economy*, Cambridge University Press, 1991; William Lazonick and Mary O'Sullivan, eds., *Corporate Governance and Sustainable Prosperity*, Palgrave, 2002; Lazonick, *Sustainable Prosperity*; Lazonick and Shin, *Predatory Value Extraction*.

[8] William Lazonick, "Is the Most Unproductive Firm the Foundation of the Most Efficient Economy? Penrosian Learning Confronts the Neoclassical Fallacy," *International Review of Applied Economics*, 36, 2, 2022: 1–32.

[9] William Lazonick, "The Theory of the Market Economy and the Social Foundations of Innovative Enterprise," *Economic and Industrial Democracy*, 24, 1, 2003: 9–44.

[10] Lazonick and Shin, *Predatory Value Extraction*.

[11] See William Lazonick, "Maximizing Shareholder Value as an Ideology of Predatory Value Extraction," in Knut Sogner and Andrea Colli, eds., *The Emergence of Corporate Governance*, Routledge, 2021: 170–186.

Business corporations provide adults in household units with employment that, with sufficient productivity, should enable them to support their families. Through formal and on-the-job training, business corporations also invest in the capabilities of people whom they employ. A corporation has an incentive to retain the people whom it has trained. It generally does so through pay increases and promotions to jobs that require superior functional capabilities and greater hierarchical responsibilities. Indeed, households' living standards rise over time primarily through augmented pay and promotions for valued employees in stable employment relations at innovative enterprises. It is through the employment relations of innovative enterprises, not labor-market supply and demand, that a nation such as the United States can generate the stable and equitable growth that supports a thriving middle class.[12]

In short, the investment triad puts in place the productive capabilities that are essential to a prosperous economy. Investments in human capabilities and physical infrastructure by household units, government agencies, and business corporations must be financed. Investments in educating the labor force and the housing stock in which families reside are generally funded by some combination of after-tax household incomes supplemented by household debt, along with government tax revenues supplemented by debt issues at the local, state, and federal levels. To some extent, business corporations finance the education of the labor force through corporate taxes, philanthropic contributions, and direct payments to employees for their own educations or their children's schooling as part of employment benefits. Corporate taxes can also be important for funding government investments in physical infrastructure.

Ultimately, the ability of household units and government agencies to afford investments in productive resources requires that business corporations utilize and further develop those investments in human capabilities and physical infrastructure. These business corporations must produce and sell competitive – high-quality, low-cost – products to survive. The innovative enterprise generates these competitive products, making it central to the triadic investment system that can put a society on a path to sustainable prosperity.

The business corporations that dominate the US economy are very large. Table 1 shows the distribution of US business-sector civilian employment by firm size for 2019. Business-sector employment is about 85 percent of total civilian employment in the US economy. In 2019, 2,230 corporations with 5,000 or more employees in the United States, with an average of 21,223 people on the payroll, accounted for 35.6 percent of all US business-sector employees and 40.7 percent of payrolls. Just 540 corporations with 20,000 or more

---

[12] Lazonick, "Labor in the Twenty-First Century"; Lazonick, "Is the Most Unproductive Firm."

Table 1 Business firms in the US economy, by establishments, employees, and payrolls, 2019

2019	Firms		Establishments		Paid employees		Annual payroll		Number of firms	Average number of employees
	Number		Number		Number		$ Billions			
All firms	6,102,412		7,959,103		132,989,428		7,429		6,102,412	22
Percent of all firms	%		%		%		%			
<5 employees	61.89		47.5		4.5		4.0		3,777,085	1.6
5–19 employees	27.11		21.4		11.5		8.4		1,654,456	9.3
20–99 employees	9.10		9.1		16.4		13.4		555,046	39
100–499 employees	1.56		4.7		14.0		13.6		94,957	196
500+ employees	0.34		17.2		53.6		60.6		20,868	3,416
5,000+ employees	0.04		11.5		35.6		40.7		2,230	21,223
10,000+ employees	0.02		9.7		29.8		33.8		1,122	35,346
20,000+ employees	0.01		7.7		23.7		26.1		540	58,357

Source: US Census Bureau, "2019 SUSB Annual Data Tables by Establishment Industry," Data and Maps, February 2022, https://www.census.gov/data/tables/2019/econ/susb/2019-susb-annual.html.

employees, averaging 58,357 employees, represented 23.7 percent of all business-sector employees and 26.1 percent of all payrolls.

The resource-allocation decisions of these large corporations have a preponderant influence on the operation and performance of the US economy, including investment in the productive capabilities of the labor force that are integral to the investment triad. In Section 2, drawing on the experience of the US economy over the past seven decades, I summarize how the United States moved toward stable and equitable growth from the late 1940s through the 1970s under a "retain-and-reinvest" corporate resource-allocation regime at major US business corporations. Companies retained a substantial portion of their profits to reinvest in the productive capabilities under their control, including those of employees, who (unlike plant and equipment) could at any point in time take their "human capital" elsewhere but who had the realistic expectation of a stable, well-paid career with one company (CWOC).

In contrast, since the early 1980s, under a "downsize-and-distribute" corporate resource-allocation regime, unstable employment, inequitable income, and sagging productivity have characterized the US economy.[13] In the transition from retain-and-reinvest to downsize-and-distribute, many of the largest, most powerful corporations have adopted a "dominate-and-distribute" regime: Based on the innovative capabilities that they have previously developed, they dominate their industries but prioritize shareholders in the allocation of corporate resources.

The practice of open-market share repurchases – aka stock buybacks – at major US business corporations has been central to the dominate-and-distribute and downsize-and-distribute regimes. Since the mid-1980s, stock buybacks have become the prime mode for the legalized looting of the business corporation. I call this looting process "predatory value extraction"[14] and contend that it is the fundamental cause of the increasing concentration of income among the richest household units and the erosion of middle-class employment opportunities for most Americans.

I conclude the Element by outlining a policy framework that, by directly confronting predatory value extraction, could stop the looting of the business corporation and put in place social institutions that support sustainable prosperity. The agenda includes (a) a ban on stock buybacks done as open-market repurchases, (b) changes in incentives for senior corporate executives that disconnect their compensation from the company's stock yields, (c) representation of workers and taxpayers as directors on corporate boards, (d) reform of the

---

[13] William Lazonick and Mary O'Sullivan, "Maximizing Shareholder Value: A New Ideology for Corporate Governance," *Economy and Society*, 29, 1, 2000: 13–35.

[14] Lazonick and Shin, *Predatory Value Extraction*.

tax system to reward innovation and penalize financialization, and, (e) guided by the investment-triad framework, government–business collaborations to support "collective and cumulative careers" of members of the US labor force. Sustained investment in human capabilities by the investment triad, including business corporations, would make it possible for an ever-increasing portion of the US labor force to engage in productive careers that underpin upward socioeconomic mobility, manifested by a growing, robust, and hopeful American middle class.

2 Innovative Enterprise

An economy cannot attain stable and equitable growth unless its major business corporations focus on investing in productive capabilities for the sake of generating higher-quality, lower-cost – that is, innovative – products. Innovative enterprise is a necessary condition for a nation's population to attain higher living standards on a sustainable basis. The innovation process that can generate a higher-quality, lower-cost product is uncertain, collective, and cumulative. Hence, a theory of innovative enterprise must comprehend these characteristics of the innovation process.[15]

- *Uncertain*: When investments in transforming technologies and accessing markets are made, the product and financial outcomes cannot be known in advance. If they were, the result would not be innovation. Hence the need for *strategy*.
- *Collective*: To generate a higher-quality, lower-cost product, the business enterprise must integrate the skills and efforts of large numbers of people with different hierarchical responsibilities and functional capabilities into the learning processes that are the essence of innovation. Hence the need for *organization*.
- *Cumulative*: Collective learning today enables collective learning tomorrow. These organizational-learning processes must be sustained continuously over time until financial returns can be generated through the sale of innovative products. Hence the need for *finance*.

Strategy, organization, and finance are generic activities in the operation of any business corporation. But it is the social content of these generic activities, embodied in distinctive social relations, that can transform the interaction of strategy, organization, and finance into innovative performance. Even a relatively

---

[15] William Lazonick, "The Theory of Innovative Enterprise: Foundations of Economic Analysis," in Thomas Clarke, Justin O'Brien, and Charles R. T. O'Kelley, eds., *The Oxford Handbook of the Corporation*, Oxford University Press, 2019: 490–514.

small company is a highly complex social organization. What I call the "social conditions of innovative enterprise" framework provides a conceptual guide to empirical company-level investigation of how a business enterprise operates and performs over time. Specifically, in the implementation of the three generic business activities, strategic control, organizational integration, and financial commitment are social conditions that can enable the corporation to manage the uncertain, collective, and cumulative character of the innovation process.

- **Strategic control**: For innovation to occur in the face of technological, market, and competitive uncertainties, executives who control corporate resource allocation must have the abilities and incentives to make strategic investments in innovation. Their abilities depend on their knowledge of how strategic investments in new productive capabilities can enhance the corporation's existing capabilities. Their incentives depend on alignment of their personal interests with the corporation's purpose of generating innovative products.
- **Organizational integration**: Implementation of an innovation strategy requires integration of people working in a complex division of labor into collective and cumulative learning processes. Work satisfaction, promotion, remuneration, and benefits are important instruments in a reward system that motivates and empowers employees to engage in collective learning over a sustained period of time.
- **Financial commitment**: For collective learning to accumulate over time, the sustained commitment of "patient capital" must keep the learning organization intact. For a young company that, because it is a "start-up," has not yet been able to turn a profit, various forms of "venture capital" can provide financial commitment. For a going concern that has achieved sustained profitability, retained earnings – leveraged, if need be, by debt issues – are the foundation of financial commitment.

The uncertainty of an innovation strategy is embodied in the fixed-cost investments required to develop the productive capabilities that may, if the strategy is successful, result in a higher-quality product. Fixed cost derives from both the size and the duration of the innovation investment strategy. If the size of investment in physical capital tends to increase the fixed cost of an innovation strategy, so too does the duration of the investment required for an organization to engage in the collective and cumulative – or organizational – learning that, by transforming technologies and accessing markets, can result in innovative products.

An innovation strategy that may eventually enable the enterprise to develop a higher-quality product may place that company at a competitive disadvantage if it only attains low levels of output. The high fixed cost of an innovation strategy creates the company's need to attain a high level of utilization of the productive resources it has developed – that is, "economies of scale." Given its existing productive capabilities, the innovating firm may experience increasing cost to maintain the productivity of variable inputs it buys as needed on the market to expand production. To overcome the constraint on its innovation strategy posed by reliance on the market to supply an input that results in increasing cost, the innovating firm integrates the production of the supply of that input into its internal operations. The development of the productive capability of this newly integrated input, however, adds to the fixed cost of the innovation strategy. The innovating firm is now under even more pressure to expand its sold output to transform high fixed cost into low unit cost.

The company's higher-quality product enables it to access a larger portion of the market than its competitors. The fixed cost of the innovation strategy depends, however, on investments in not only transforming technology but also accessing markets. Besides distribution facilities, accessing a larger market share may entail fixed costs for branding, advertising, distribution channels, and a salaried sales force. Learning about what potential buyers want, and convincing potential buyers that the company's product is actually "higher quality," add to the fixed cost of the innovation strategy.

Indeed, in some industries, the fixed cost of accessing a larger market share is greater than the fixed cost of investing in the transformation of product and process technologies. An increase in fixed cost of accessing the market requires an even larger extent of the market to convert high fixed cost into low unit cost. A potent way for an innovating firm to attain a larger extent of the market is for the company to share some of the gains of this cost transformation with its customers in the form of a lower product price.

Along with investment in plant and equipment, investment in productive resources entails training and retaining employees. When a company enhances an employee's productive capability, through either formal or on-the-job training, the employee's upgraded capability represents a fixed-cost asset that can improve the quality of the innovating firm's product, which in turn can enable the company to attain a larger extent of the market to transform the increased fixed cost of its investment in human resources into low unit cost. When the company succeeds in generating a higher-quality, lower-cost product, innovation drives its growth.

To retain and motivate the employees whom the company has hired and trained, the innovating firm can offer them higher pay, more employment security, superior benefits, and more interesting work, all of which add to the fixed cost of the asset that an employee's labor represents. If these rewards to employees result in innovative products, the gains of employees may represent contributions to value creation that make the company an even more profitable business enterprise. The innovating firm shares the gains of innovation with its employees by making investments in what I have called their "collective and cumulative careers." Individuals develop their own productive capabilities as members of collectivities organized by the corporation (in some cases in collaboration with other business corporations or with government agencies). And the specialized knowledge that enables individuals to become more productive over time cumulates through their ongoing involvement in collective learning processes. Over the course of their careers, individuals may change employers, making it necessary for them to engage in collective and cumulative learning, in a coherent and continuous manner, across a series of business, government, and civil-society organizations.

Career employees, therefore, can become more productive because of their sustained involvement in processes of collective and cumulative learning.[16] In rewarding employees for this engagement, the innovating firm makes its employees better off. It can afford, and indeed profit from, the increased labor expense when the employee's productive capability enables the company to gain a competitive advantage by generating higher-quality, lower-cost products than had previously been available. Under such circumstances, increases in labor income and increases in labor productivity tend to show a highly positive correlation.

When the innovating firm is successful, it may come to dominate its industry. The company's output is far larger and its unit cost, and hence potentially its product price, is far lower than would be the case if a large number of small firms with lower-quality products and lesser-scale economies populated the industry. The overall gains from innovation depend on the relation between the innovating firm's cost structure and the industry's demand structure, while the distribution of those gains among the company's various stakeholders depends on their relative power to appropriate portions of these gains.[17]

It is theoretically possible (although by no means inevitable) for the gains of an innovative enterprise to permit, simultaneously, higher pay, more stable employment, and better work conditions for its employees; a stronger balance sheet for the firm; more secure paper for creditors; higher dividends and stock prices for shareholders; more tax revenues for governments; and higher-quality

---

[16] Lazonick et al., "Skill Development"; Matt Hopkins and William Lazonick, "Who Invests in the High-Tech Knowledge Base?" Institute for New Economic Thinking, Working Group on the Political Economy of Distribution Working Paper No. 14, May 2014, https://www.ineteco nomics.org/research/research-papers/who-invests-in-the-high-tech-knowledge-base.

[17] William Lazonick, *Competitive Advantage on the Shop Floor*, Harvard University Press, 1990; Lazonick, "The Theory of Innovative Enterprise."

products at lower prices for consumers. To some extent, what is theoretically possible has been, in certain times and places, historical reality. In the rise of the United States to global industrial leadership during the twentieth century, a retain-and-reinvest resource-allocation regime enabled a relatively small number of business enterprises in a wide range of industries to grow to employ tens of thousands, or even hundreds of thousands, of people and attain dominant product-market shares.[18]

The fifty largest US industrial corporations by revenues in 1957 averaged 87,080 employees worldwide in 1957, 117,393 in 1967, and 119,093 in 1977. In total, these fifty companies employed 4.4 million people worldwide in 1957, 5.9 million in 1967, and 6.0 million in 1977. Table 2 shows the changes in employment over this period for the twenty largest employers in both 1957 and 1977. These twenty companies employed 3.1 million people worldwide in 1957, 3.8 million in 1967, and 4.0 million in 1977.

The sectors with the largest employers included automobiles, tires, steel, electrical machinery, electronics, aerospace, oil refining, and chemicals. Over this period, as it became the world's dominant computer company, IBM increased its employment five-fold, rising from the twenty-fourth largest employer in 1957 to the fifth largest in 1977.

Not all the top twenty companies in 1957 increased their employment over the subsequent two decades. The two steel companies in Table 2 downsized substantially from the 1950s to the 1970s, while the two aircraft manufacturing companies had highly cyclical employment, with Douglas having a huge increase in its labor force when it merged with McDonnell in 1967. Two companies, ITT and Gulf & Western, grew to be very large during the 1960s conglomerate movement, which in historical retrospect represented the first important stage in the financialization of the US corporate economy, with corporate growth being driven by acquisition of companies in industries that were unrelated to one another in terms of technologies or markets.[19]

Notwithstanding conglomeration, most of the companies in Table 2 were in retain-and-reinvest mode during these two decades. Companies retained corporate profits and reinvested them in productive capabilities, including processes of collective and cumulative learning. Companies integrated personnel into learning processes through career employment. Into the 1980s, the norm of

---

[18] Alfred D. Chandler, Jr., *The Visible Hand: The Managerial Revolution in American Business*, Harvard University Press, 1977; Alfred D. Chandler, Jr., *Scale and Scope: The Dynamics of Industrial Capitalism*, Harvard University Press, 1990; William Lazonick, "Corporate Restructuring," in Stephen Ackroyd, Rose Batt, Paul Thompson, and Pamela Tolbert, eds., *The Oxford Handbook of Work and Organization*, Oxford University Press, 2004: 577–601; Lazonick, *Sustainable Prosperity*, Chs. 2 and 3.
[19] Lazonick, "Corporate Restructuring."

Table 2 Worldwide corporate employment, 1957–1977, twenty largest US-based industrial employers in 1957 and 1977

Company	Rank 1957	1957	1962	1967	1972	1977	Rank 1977
General Motors	1	588,160	604,278	728,198	759,543	797,000	1
General Electric	2	282,029	258,174	375,000	369,000	384,000	3
US Steel	3	271,037	194,044	197,643	176,486	165,845	8
Ford Motor	4	191,759	302,563	394,323	442,607	479,000	2
Bethlehem Steel	5	166,859	122,089	131,000	109,000	94,000	22
Standard Oil (Standard Oil (NJ)/Exxon)[1]	6	160,000	150,000	150,000	141,000	127,000	14
Western Electric	7	144,055	151,174	169,700	205,665	162,000	9
Chrysler	8	136,187	77,194[2]	215,907	244,844	250,833	6
Westinghouse Electric	9	128,572	109,966	132,049	183,768	141,394	11
ITT	10	128,000	157,000	236,000	428,000	375,000	4
Goodyear Rubber and Tire	11	101,386	95,740	113,207	145,201	159,890	10
Boeing	12	94,998	104,100	142,700	58,600	66,900	42
Sperry Rand	13	93,130	103,545	101,603	85,574	85,684	28
General Dynamics	14	91,700	84,500	103,196	60,900	73,268	36
Du Pont (E.I.) de Nemours	15	90,088	93,159	111,931	111,052	131,317	13
Firestone Tire & Rubber	16	88,323	83,909	95,500	109,000	115,000	18
Douglas/McDonnell Douglas[3]	17	78,400	44,000	140,050	86,713	61,577	47

Table 2 (cont.)

Company	Rank 1957	1957	1962	1967	1972	1977	Rank 1977
RCA	18	78,000	87,000	128,000	122,000	111,000	20
Socony Mobil Oil/Mobil Oil/Mobil[4]	19	77,000	74,900	75,800	75,400	200,700	7
Swift/Esmark[5]	20	71,900	54,200	48,300	33,600	44,700	85
Other companies among top 20 employers in 1977							
IBM	26	60,281	81,493	221,866	262,152	310,155	5
United Aircraft/United Technologies[6]	24	61,688	63,461	78,743	63,849	138,587	12
Eastman Kodak	37	50,300	47,800	105,600	114,800	123,700	15
Gulf & Western Industries[7]	na	na	na	46,000	65,000	116,600	16
North Amer. Aviation/Rockwell Int'l.[8]	30	54,660	97,728	115,326	80,045	115,162	17
Union Carbide	23	64,247	58,798	99,794	98,114	113,669	19

Notes: [1]Standard Oil of New Jersey (Esso) changed its name to Exxon from 1972. [2]US employment only. [3]Douglas Aircraft merged with McDonnell Aircraft in 1967 to form McDonnell Douglas. [4]Socony Mobil Oil changed its name to Mobil Oil in 1966, and then to Mobil in 1976. [5]Swift became the core company of Esmark in 1977. [6]United Aircraft changed its name to United Technologies in 1975. [7]Originating as a Michigan autoparts distributor, Gulf & Western Industries acquired Paramount Pictures in 1966 and became a major conglomerate. [8]The 1967 merger of North American Aviation and Rockwell-Standard created North American Rockwell, renamed Rockwell International in 1973.

Sources: "Fortune 500," *Fortune*, June 1958, July 1963, June 1968, May 1973, May 1978.

a "career with one company" prevailed at major US corporations.[20] A steady stream of dividend income out of profits and the prospect of higher future stock prices based on the next generation of innovative products gave shareholders an interest in retain-and-reinvest.

In the immediate post–World War II decades, the beneficiaries of a retain-and-reinvest corporate resource-allocation regime, with its CWOC norm, were mainly white males, be they high-school-educated blue-collar workers or college-educated white-collar workers. At the blue-collar level, the presence of industrial unions helped to ensure that employees would experience employment stability and income equity. At the white-collar level, when a company trained employees early in their careers, it sought to retain them by offering the promise of a career with the company, topped off with healthcare coverage and a corporation-funded, nonportable defined-benefit pension based on the employee's years of service.

For minorities and women, who had been largely left out of this postwar CWOC bargain, access to more stable employment and more equitable income was supported by the Civil Rights Act of 1964 and the launch of the Equal Employment Opportunity Commission (EEOC) the following year. At that point, it was assumed that the surest path to upward socioeconomic mobility for both blue-collar and white-collar workers was through career employment in one of the major business corporations that dominated the US economy.[21] This CWOC norm was, for example, the point of departure for a thirty-one-volume study, *The Racial Policies of American Industry* (RPAI), carried out at Wharton in the last half of the 1960s and early 1970s, on the implementation of equal employment opportunity, with a focus on upward mobility along hierarchical job structures within major business corporations.[22]

In a project supported by the Institute for New Economic Thinking, Philip Moss, Joshua Weitz, and I have documented in detail how by the 1970s hundreds of thousands of African Americans with no more than high-school

---

[20] Lazonick, *Sustainable Prosperity,* Ch. 3.

[21] William Lazonick, Philip Moss, and Joshua Weitz, "The Equal Employment Opportunity Omission," Institute for New Economic Thinking Working Paper No. 53, December 5, 2016, https://www.ineteconomics.org/research/research-papers/the-equal-employment-opportunity-omission; Lazonick et al., "How the Disappearance of Unionized Jobs Obliterated an Emergent Black Middle Class."

[22] For the thinking underpinning the RPAI study, see Herbert R. Northrup and Richard L. Rowan, *The Negro and Employment Opportunity: Problems and Practices*, The University of Michigan, 1965, pp. v–x. For a summary of its arguments and evidence, see Joshua Weitz, William Lazonick, and Philip Moss, "Employment Mobility and the Belated Emergence of the Black Middle Class," Institute for New Economic Thinking Working Paper No. 143, January 2, 2021, https://www.ineteconomics.org/research/research-papers/employment-mobility-and-the-belated-emergence-of-the-black-middle-class.

diplomas were attaining middle-class status through employment in unionized semi-skilled jobs in mass-production industries such as automobiles, steel, and electronics manufacturing. As a result, a Black blue-collar middle class began to emerge.[23] During this period, however, white males maintained privileged access to intergenerational upward mobility from blue-collar jobs to white-collar jobs as the sons of blue-collar workers obtained higher educations followed by CWOC white-collar employment in business corporations.

In the 1970s, females with college educations (disproportionately white) also gained significantly increased access to career employment in business corporations. Their upward mobility was obstructed, however, by the persistence of the "glass ceiling," set in place by the ideology that they would give up or interrupt their careers when children arrived in order to assume the traditional middle-class "stay-at-home-mother" role.[24] Thus, even women who chose not to have children, or who had household arrangements for childcare that enabled them to devote themselves to careers in business corporations or government agencies, continued to face gender discrimination based on presumptions concerning the household division of labor.

From the late 1970s and continuing to the present, however, for masses of Americans, including white males, the quantity and quality of employment opportunities that could support upward mobility within major business corporations have eroded, while the distribution of income within the companies has grown increasingly unequal.[25] By the first half of the 1980s, some acute observers of blue-collar employment relations perceived that the US income distribution was taking a "great U-turn."[26] In retrospect, we now know that since that change in direction in the early 1980s, the United States has continued down the road to extreme income inequality and the erosion of middle-class employment opportunity. The social-conditions framework provides insights into this historic change in the direction of US economic performance – essentially the end of the national quest for sustainable prosperity – by focusing on

---

[23] Weitz et al., "Employment Mobility"; William Lazonick, Philip Moss, and Joshua Weitz, "The Unmaking of the Black Blue-Collar Middle Class," Institute for New Economic Thinking Working Paper No. 159, May 20, 2021, www.ineteconomics.org/research/research-papers/the-unmaking-of-the-black-blue-collar-middle-class.

[24] Alison M. Conrad and Kathy Cannings, "Sex Segregation in the Workplace and the Mommy Track," *Academy of Management Proceedings*, 1, 1990.

[25] William Lazonick, Philip Moss, and Joshua Weitz, "Equality Denied: Tech and African Americans," Institute for New Economic Thinking Working Paper No. 177, February 18, 2022, https://www.ineteconomics.org/research/research-papers/equality-denied-tech-and-african-americans.

[26] Bennett Harrison and Barry Bluestone, *The Great U-Turn: Corporate Restructuring and the Polarizing of America*, Basic Books, 1986; Bennett Harrison, Chris Tilly, and Barry Bluestone, "Wage Inequality Takes a Great U-Turn," *Challenge*, 29, 1, 1986: 26–32.

the transformation of the dominant regime of resource allocation among major US industrial corporations from retain-and-reinvest to downsize-and-distribute.

3 From Retain-and-Reinvest to Downsize-and-Distribute

Under a retain-and-reinvest regime, the corporation retains earnings and reinvests them in the productive capabilities of its labor force. Under downsize-and-distribute, the corporation lays off experienced, often more expensive, workers and distributes corporate cash to shareholders.[27] Since the beginning of the 1980s, employment relations in US industrial corporations have undergone three major structural changes, summarized as "rationalization," "marketization," and "globalization," by means of which corporations have downsized their US labor forces, resulting in downward rather than upward socioeconomic mobility.[28]

From the early 1980s, *rationalization*, characterized by plant closings, terminated the jobs of high-school-educated blue-collar workers, most of them well-paid union members. From the early 1990s, marketization, characterized by the end of a CWOC as an employment norm, placed in jeopardy the job security of middle-aged white-collar workers, many of them college educated. From the early 2000s, *globalization*, characterized by the accelerated movement of even advanced employment opportunities offshore to lower-wage nations, especially China and India, left all members of the US labor force vulnerable to displacement, whatever their educational credentials and work experience.[29]

As documented in my book, *Sustainable Prosperity in the New Economy?*, the offshoring of employment in the information-and-communication-technology (ICT) industries had begun in the 1960s and was operating on a large scale in the context of the microelectronics revolution of the 1980s and 1990s. Most of the offshoring through the 1980s was to gain access to low wage but literate female labor for testing and assembling of semiconductors and other electronics components in Hong Kong, Singapore, South Korea, Taiwan, and Malaysia. US multinational electronics companies employed indigenous engineers and managers (all males) to run these Asian plants, thus launching many technology and management careers in those nations.

Large numbers of young Asians with undergraduate degrees, especially in science and engineering, also came to the United States for graduate education and work experience. During the 1990s, there was an enormous increase in the employment of college-educated Asians, particularly from India and China, by

---

[27] Lazonick and O'Sullivan, "Maximizing Shareholder Value."
[28] Lazonick, "Labor in the Twenty-First Century"; Lazonick et al., "The Equal Employment Opportunity Omission."
[29] See William Lazonick, *Sustainable Prosperity in the New Economy?*, Ch. 5.

ICT companies operating in the United States under H-1B, L-1, and employment-based permanent-resident visas. By the 2000s, highly educated Asians had become central to the competitive capabilities of US-based ICT companies.[30] Large numbers of these personnel, however, also returned to their home nations, especially China and India, armed with more education and experience, to contribute to the upgrading of global value chains and engage in indigenous innovation.[31]

Initially, structural changes in employment through rationalization, marketization, and globalization were business responses to changes in technologies, markets, and competition. During the onset of the rationalization phase in the early 1980s, plant closings as well as cost-cutting by offshoring component manufacture were reactions to the superior productive capabilities of Japanese competitors in consumer-durable and related capital-goods industries in which US companies employed large numbers of unionized blue-collar workers. During the onset of the marketization phase in the early 1990s, the erosion of the CWOC norm among white-collar workers was a response to the dramatic technological shift from proprietary systems to open systems, integral to the microelectronics revolution. This shift favored younger workers with the latest computer skills acquired through higher education and transferable across companies over older workers with many years of firm-specific experience. During the onset of the globalization phase in the early 2000s, the sharp acceleration in the offshoring of high-end jobs was a response to the emergence of large supplies of highly educated but lower-wage labor in developing nations such as China and India. Linked to the United States through inexpensive communication and transportation networks, this alternative labor pool could perform increasingly sophisticated activities that had previously been carried out in the United States.[32]

Once US corporations transformed their employment relations, they often pursued rationalization, marketization, and globalization to cut current costs

---

[30] Lazonick et al., "Equality Denied: Tech and African Americans."

[31] Qiwen Lu, *China's Leap into the Information Age: Innovation and Organization in the Computer industry*, Oxford University Press, 2000; William Lazonick, "Indigenous Innovation and Economic Development: Lessons from China's Leap into the Information Age," *Industry & Innovation*, 11, 4, 2004: 273–298; Yu Zhou, William Lazonick, and Yifei Sun, eds., *China as an Innovation Nation*, Oxford University Press, 2016; Kaidong Feng, *Innovation and Industrial Development in China: A Schumpeterian Perspective on China's Economic Transformation*, Routledge, 2020; Yin Li and William Lazonick, "China's Development Path: Government, Business, and Globalization in an Innovating Economy," Institute for New Economic Thinking Working Paper No. 190, August 11, 2022, https://www.ineteconomics.org/research/research-papers/chinas-development-path-government-business-and-globalization-in-an-innovating-economy.

[32] Lazonick, *Sustainable Prosperity*, Ch. 5.

rather than to reposition their organizations to produce innovative products. Corporate profits ceased to provide funds for reinvesting in the growth of the firm and instead became "free cash flow" that could be distributed to shareholders to "maximize shareholder value." Defining superior corporate performance as ever-higher quarterly earnings per share, companies turned to massive open-market stock repurchases to "manage" their own corporations' stock prices. Trillions of dollars that could have been spent on investment in productive capabilities in the US economy since the mid-1980s have been used instead to buy back corporate shares for the purpose of manipulating stock prices.[33]

In 1997, buybacks first surpassed dividends in the US corporate economy, and have far exceeded them in recent stock-market booms.[34] As a form of distribution to shareholders, buybacks done as open-market repurchases are much more volatile than dividends, with buybacks booming when stock prices are high. As Figure 1 shows, since the early 1980s, major US corporations have been doing stock buybacks in addition to (not instead of) making dividend payments to shareholders.

Figure 1 charts dividends and buybacks for the 216 companies included in the S&P 500 Index in January 2020 that were publicly listed from 1981 through 2019. Coming into the 1980s, buybacks were minimal, and from 1981 to 1983, buybacks for these 216 companies absorbed only 4.4 percent of net income, with dividends representing 49.7 percent. From 2017 to 2019, buybacks for the same 216 companies were *62.2 percent* of net income and dividends 49.6 percent.

Table 3 displays the data on buybacks and dividends in Figure 1 as percentages of net income for the 216 companies for 1981–1984 – just before and after the adoption of SEC Rule 10b-18 gave US business corporations a "license to loot"[35] – and then for five-year periods from 1985 to 1989 through 2015–2019. The proportions for 2005–2009 and 2015–2019 capture the surges in buybacks during years in which, except for 2008 and 2009, profits were high and the stock market was booming. From 2003 to 2007, the value of buybacks done by S&P 500 Index companies quadrupled. In general, these publicly listed companies have done

---

[33] William Lazonick, "Stock Buybacks: From Retain-and-Reinvest to Downsize-and-Distribute," Center for Effective Public Management, Brookings Institution, April 2015, https://www.brookings.edu/research/stock-buybacks-from-retain-and-reinvest-to-downsize-and-distribute/;
William Lazonick, "The Value-Extracting CEO: How Executive Stock-Based Pay Undermines Investment in Productive Capabilities," *Structural Change and Economic Dynamics*, 48, 2019: 53–68.

[34] Lazonick, "Stock Buybacks," pp. 10–11.

[35] William Lazonick and Ken Jacobson, "Letter to SEC: How Stock Buybacks Undermine Investment in Innovation for the Sake of Stock-Price Manipulation," *Institute for New Economic Thinking*, April 1, 2022, https://www.ineteconomics.org/perspectives/blog/letter-to-sec-a-policy-framework-for-attaining-sustainable-prosperity-in-the-united-states.

Table 3 Cash dividends (DV) and stock buybacks (BB) as percentages of net income (NI), 1981–2019, for the 216 business corporations in the S&P 500 Index in January 2020 that were publicly listed for all thirty-nine years

	1981–1984	1985–1989	1990–1994	1995–1999	2000–2004	2005–2009	2010–2014	2015–2019
DV/NI%	48.3	50.3	53.9	37.0	40.5	40.7	35.7	50.5
BB/NI%	8.6	29.5	20.5	40.7	38.0	54.8	44.3	61.7
(DV+BB)/NI%	56.9	79.8	74.4	77.7	78.4	95.5	80.0	112.2

Source: S&P Compustat database and company 10-K filings, compiled by Mustafa Erdem Sakinç and Emre Gömeç of the Academic-Industry Research Network.

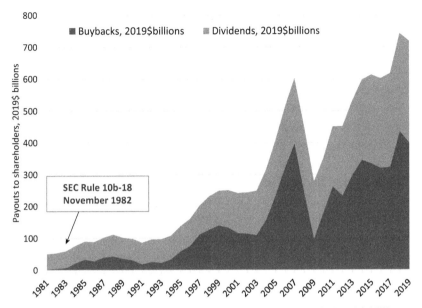

Figure 1 Stock buybacks and cash dividends, 1981–2019, in 2019$ billion, for the 216 business corporations in the S&P 500 Index in January 2020 that were publicly listed for all thirty-nine years

Source: S&P Compustat database and company 10-K filings, compiled by Mustafa Erdem Sakinç and Emre Gömeç of the Academic-Industry Research Network.

buybacks when stock prices have been high and rising, as they have competed with one another to give manipulative boosts to their stock prices. These data show that even as buybacks have absorbed a large proportion of net income, these companies have paid ample dividends. The half-decade 2015–2019 is particularly noteworthy for the extent of distributions to shareholders in the years preceding the onset of the Covid-19 pandemic.[36]

For the decade 2012–2021, 474 corporations that were included in the S&P 500 Index in January 2022 repurchased shares valued at $5.7 trillion, equal to 55 percent of their net income, while also paying out $4.2 trillion in dividends, another 41 percent of net income.[37] These distributions to shareholders come at the expense of rewards to employees in the form of higher pay, superior benefits,

---

[36] William Lazonick, Mustafa Erdem Sakinç, and Matt Hopkins, "Why Stock Buybacks Are Dangerous for the Economy," *Harvard Business Review*, January 7, 2020, https://hbr.org/2020/01/why-stock-buybacks-are-dangerous-for-the-economy?ab=hero-subleft-; William Lazonick and Matt Hopkins, "How 'Maximizing Shareholder Value' Minimized the Strategic National Stockpile," Institute for New Economic Thinking Working Paper No. 127, July 21, 2020, https://papers.ssrn.com/sol3/papers.cfm?abstract_id=3671025.

[37] Database compiled by Öner Tulum of the Academic-Industry Research Network from S&P Compustat and corporate 10-K filings with the Securities and Exchange Commission.

and more secure jobs as well as corporate investment in the new products and processes that can sustain a company as an innovative enterprise. These distributions are a prime cause of the concentration of income among the richest households and the erosion of middle-class employment opportunities.[38] Massive payouts in the form of buybacks and dividends are also integral to resource-allocation strategies that have caused US corporations to fall behind global competitors in major technology sectors, including ICT, pharmaceuticals, and aviation – sectors in which the United States once possessed world leadership.[39]

As these data on distributions to shareholders show, since the mid-1980s, among corporations listed on US stock markets – of which the New York Stock Exchange (NYSE) and the National Association of Securities Dealers Automated Quotation (NASDAQ) system are by far the most important – trillions of dollars have been extracted from business corporations in the form of stock buybacks in addition to dividends. The two types of distributions to shareholders both drain corporate treasuries, but they differ in terms of how the gains from them are realized and the implications for corporate investment in productive capabilities. Shareholders who purchase shares of a company on the stock exchange can get a dividend yield on that portfolio investment by *holding* shares. Open-market repurchases (representing the vast majority of buybacks), in contrast, increase the gains of *sharesellers* who, as professional stock traders, are in the business of timing the buying and selling of shares, often benefiting from access to nonpublic information on the precise days on which the company is executing buybacks. These privileged sharesellers include senior executives of the company doing the buybacks, Wall Street bankers, and hedge-fund managers.[40]

Stable shareholders who buy corporate stocks for dividend yields should be opposed to buybacks. Instead, they should want corporate management to reinvest in the productive capabilities of the company as a basis for creating

---

[38] Lazonick, "Labor in the Twenty-First Century"; Lazonick, "The Value-Extracting CEO."

[39] See Öner Tulum and William Lazonick, "Financialized Corporations in a National Innovation System: The US Pharmaceutical Industry," *International Journal of Political Economy*, 47, 3–4, 2018: 281–316; William Lazonick and Mustafa Erdem Sakinç, "Make Passengers Safer? Boeing Just Made Shareholders Richer," *American Prospect*, May 31, 2019, https://prospect.org/envir onment/make-passengers-safer-boeing-just-made-shareholders-richer./; William Lazonick and Matt Hopkins, "Why the CHIPS Are Down: Stock Buybacks and Subsidies in the U.S. Semiconductor Industry," Institute for New Economic Thinking Working Paper No. 165, November 1, 2021, www.ineteconomics.org/research/research-papers/why-the-chips-are-down-stock-buybacks-and-subsidies-in-the-u-s-semiconductor-industry; Marie Carpenter and William Lazonick, "The Pursuit of Shareholder Value: Cisco's Transformation from Innovation to Financialization," Institute for New Economic Thinking Working Paper No. 202, February 21, 2023, https://www.ineteconomics.org/research/research-papers/the-pursuit-of-shareholder-value-ciscos-transformation-from-innovation-to-financialization.

[40] Lazonick and Shin, *Predatory Value Extraction*.

the next round of competitive products that can generate the profits out of which a stream of dividends can continue to be paid. If the company is successful in making these investments in innovation, its shares should rise in value, giving shareholders a capital gain if and when they decide to sell some or all of their shares.

Why, then, are companies doing these massive distributions to shareholders? In my article "Profits Without Prosperity: Stock Buybacks Manipulate the Market and Leave Most Americans Worse Off," published in *Harvard Business Review* in 2014,[41] I argue that the stock-based remuneration of senior executives who exercise strategic control over resource allocation in these US business corporations incentivizes them to manipulate their companies' stock prices. Figure 2 shows the average total compensation of the 500 highest-paid executives in the United States in each year from 2006 to 2021, ranging from $15.9 million in 2009, of which, even with the stock market depressed, stock-based pay was 60.2 percent of the total, to $47.4 million in 2021, of which, with the stock market booming, stock-based pay was 88.2 percent of the total.

Stock-based pay mainly takes the form of stock options and stock awards. Stock options were much more widely used than stock awards in the 1990s. Since the mid-2000s, stock awards have increased in popularity, largely because, in the context of new rules that require companies to expense stock-based pay on their financial statements, awards require fewer shares than options to generate the same realized gains from stock-based pay.[42] In 2006, with the average total compensation of the 500 highest-paid executives at $25.6 million, realized gains from stock options represented 56 percent of the total, while realized gains from stock awards represented 17 percent. In 2021, with the average total compensation of the 500 highest-paid executives at $47.4 million, realized gains from stock options were 44.2 percent and realized gains from stock awards were 44.0 percent. This stock-based pay incentivizes US corporate executives to boost their companies' stock prices and amply rewards them for doing so. In stock buybacks, they have at their disposal an instrument to "maximize shareholder value" and, in the process, enrich themselves. In their massive and widespread use of this instrument, senior corporate executives have been participating in the looting of the US business corporation.[43]

---

[41] William Lazonick, "Profits Without Prosperity: Stock Buybacks Manipulate the Market and Leave Most Americans Worse Off," *Harvard Business Review*, September 2014: 46–55, https://hbr.org/2014/09/profits-without-prosperity; see also Lazonick, "Stock Buybacks"; Lazonick, "The Value-Extracting CEO."

[42] Matt Hopkins and William Lazonick, *Executive Pay: Incentives for Innovation or Financialization?* Cambridge Elements: Corporate Governance, Cambridge University Press, forthcoming 2023.

[43] Lazonick, "The Value-Extracting CEO."

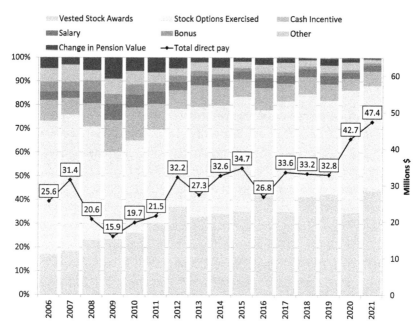

Figure 2 Average total remuneration ($ millions) and its proportional components, 500 highest-paid executives of US business corporations in each year, 2006–2021 (total direct pay labels in $ millions)

Notes: Vested stock awards and stock options exercised are realized gains from these two types of stock-based compensation. Omitted from these averages are the following executives whose extraordinarily high remuneration in certain years would have, if included, significantly skewed the results: 2012, Mark Zuckerberg ($2.3 billion), Richard Kinder ($1.1 billion); 2013, Mark Zuckerberg ($3.3 billion); 2016, Elon Musk ($1.3 billion); 2021, Elon Musk ($23.5 billion).

Source: S&P ExecuComp database, calculations by Matt Hopkins of the Academic-Industry Research Network.

Senior corporate executives have embraced shareholder-value ideology since the late 1980s, but they have not acted alone. In *Predatory Value Extraction*, Jang-Sup Shin and I classify senior executives as value-extracting *insiders*, asset managers (aka institutional shareholders) as value-extracting *enablers*, and shareholder (aka hedge-fund) activists as value-extracting *outsiders*.[44] As we detail in our book and as I summarize in the concluding section of this Element, there now exists in the United States a corrupt proxy-voting system that obliges asset-fund managers to vote the proxies for the stocks in their securities portfolios, enabling shareholder activists with a stake of, say, 1 percent of a company's outstanding

---

[44] Lazonick and Shin, *Predatory Value Extraction*.

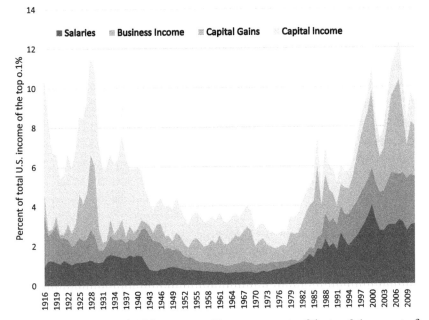

Figure 3 Share of total US incomes and its components of the top 0.1 percent of households in the US income distribution, 1916–2011

Notes: The category "salaries" includes compensation from realized gains on exercising stock options and the vesting of stock awards. The data are not available in categories that permit the extension of this analysis of the components of the pay of the top 0.1 percent beyond 2011.

Source: F. Alvaredo, T. Atkinson, T. Piketty, and E. Saez, "The World Top Incomes Database," Paris School of Economics, www.parisschoolofeconomics.eu/en/news/the-top-incomes-database-new-website/ (top 0.1 percent income composition, 2011).

shares to assert immense pressure on corporate executives and directors to engage in downsize-and-distribute.

The stock-based pay of US corporate executives is an important reason for the extreme concentration of income that has occurred since the 1980s among the richest households in the United States. Based on data from household federal tax filings, Figure 3 shows the share of income in the hands of 0.1 percent of all households with the highest incomes, including capital gains, from 1916 to 2011. In 1975, the share of the top 0.1 percent was 2.56 percent of all US incomes, the lowest proportion over the entire ninety-six-year period. The highest proportion was 12.28 percent in 2007, just before the financial crisis. During the 2008 stock-market crisis, the share of the top 0.1 percent declined, but with the recovery, their share bounced back. In 2012 (not included in Figure 3), the share of the top

0.1 percent was 11.33 percent, the fourth highest proportion recorded.[45] Clearly, from the late 1970s, on a dramatic scale, there was a reversal in the trend toward a somewhat falling share of income of the top 0.1 percent that had occurred in the decades after World War II.

Note that in Figure 3 a large part of the explosion of the share of the top 0.1 percent was in the form of "salaries," which includes *realized gains from stock-based pay* (stock options and stock awards) that appeared in the summary statistics of an executive's Form 1040 tax returns (the source of these data) as "Wages, salaries, tips, etc." Since 1976, virtually all realized gains from stock-based pay have been taxed at the ordinary income tax rates and hence are not included in the capital-gains portion of the incomes of the top 0.1 percent as shown in Figure 3.

Top executives of US business corporations, both industrial and financial, are well represented among the top 0.1 percent of the US income distribution, with much, and often most, of their compensation coming from realized gains from exercising stock options and the vesting of stock awards. When this mode of compensating top executives is combined with the fact that Wall Street has, since the 1980s, judged the performance of corporations by their quarterly stock yields, the importance of stock-based pay in executive compensation is clear. Stock-based pay gives top executives powerful personal incentives to boost, from quarter to quarter, the stock prices of the companies that employ them. In stock buybacks, these executives have found a potent instrument for stock-market manipulation from which they can benefit personally, even if the stock-price boosts are only temporary.

Most household income comes from working in paid employment. Figure 4 shows the relation between the cumulative increase in hourly labor productivity and the cumulative increase in real hourly wages in the business sector of the US economy from 1948 to 2021. From the late 1940s to the mid-1970s, rates of increase in real wages kept up with rates of increase in labor productivity – an indicator of "shared prosperity."[46] The prime reason for the trend toward more

---

[45] Facundo Alvaredo, Anthony B. Atkinson, Thomas Piketty, and Emmanuel Saez, "The World Top Incomes Database," *Paris School of Economics*, https://www.parisschoolofeconomics.eu/en/news/the-top-incomes-database-new-website/.

[46] The Gini coefficient for US households also shows a trend toward a somewhat more equal distribution of income in the post–World War II followed by a sharp reversal in the early 1980s, with persistent and ever-more extreme increases in income inequality to the present. US Census Bureau, "Income Gini Ratio of Families by Race of Householder, All Races [GINIALLRF]," FRED, Federal Reserve Bank of St. Louis, September 21, 2022, https://fred.stlouisfed.org/series/GINIALLRF. See also David Leonhardt, "Our Broken Economy, in One Simple Chart," *New York Times*, August 7, 2017, www.nytimes.com/interactive/2017/08/07/opinion/leonhardt-income-inequality.html, which uses US federal income-tax data to show that households lower in the income distribution in 1980 had higher gains income growth from 1946 to 1980, whereas the

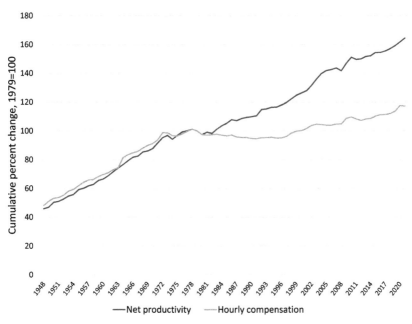

Figure 4 Index of cumulative annual percent changes in productivity per hour and real wages per hour (1979 = 100), 1948–2021

Source: Economic Policy Institute, "The Productivity-Pay Gap," October 2022, https://www.epi.org/productivity-pay-gap/.

equality was the retain-and-reinvest regime of corporate resource allocation that prevailed in the post–World War II era, characterized by CWOC employment relations.[47] From the late 1970s, however, the productivity-growth rate began to outstrip the wage-growth rate, and over the ensuing decades, the gap between the two grew wider and wider, as shown in Figure 4.

In the late 1970s, the gap appeared as corporations looked for ways to suppress wage growth as profits were being eroded by inflation. During the following decades, the transformation of corporate employment relations through rationalization, marketization, and globalization served to widen the productivity-pay gap. In terms of the actual distribution of income, however, this gap resulted not only from the power of major corporations to suppress wages but also the siphoning of corporate productivity gains, amounting to trillions upon trillions of dollars, to shareholders in the form of dividends and

---

very richest households in the income distribution in 2014 had most of the gains in income growth from 1980 to 2014.

[47] Lazonick, "Labor in the Twenty-First Century"; Lazonick et al., "The Equal Employment Opportunity Omission."

buybacks.[48] Of particular importance to the distribution of corporate income between employees and shareholders is Rule 10b-18, adopted by the SEC under the radar in November 1982. Rule 10b-18 transformed the SEC from a body that is supposed to mitigate stock-market manipulation to one that actively encourages it.[49]

4 Shareholder-Value Ideology and the Looting of the US Business Corporation

Stock buybacks incentivized by the stock-based pay of senior executives are the clearest manifestations of the financialization of the US business corporation. This financialized mode of corporate resource allocation has been legitimized by the ideology that a business corporation should be run to "maximize shareholder value" (MSV). Through stock options and stock awards, corporate executives who make the resource-allocation decisions to distribute cash to shareholders are themselves prime beneficiaries of the focus on rising stock prices, earnings per share, and total shareholder yield (dividends plus stock-price gains) as the sole measures of corporate performance. As rationalization, marketization, and globalization have undermined stable and remunerative employment structures, the financialization of the US corporation has entailed the distribution of corporate cash to shareholders through stock repurchases, usually in addition to generous cash dividends. Over the past two decades, at an accelerating rate, hedge-fund activists have joined senior corporate executives in the feeding frenzy in a process that can only be described as the legalized looting of the US business corporation.[50]

The dramatic change in trajectory from retain-and-reinvest to downsize-and-distribute that has occurred in the United States over the past four decades did not have to happen. Rather, it was imposed upon the US labor force by the dominance of a highly damaging and fallacious ideology of the relation between corporate governance and economic performance. In the name of MSV, US business executives have favored extracting value that workers have already created while also neglecting to invest in productive capabilities that can enable workers to create new sources of value in the future. In so doing, they have

---

[48] A 105-page paper on the evolution of wage suppression and wage inequality in the United States by the Economic Policy Institute, originator of the "productivity-pay gap" metric, makes no mention of stock buybacks as a cause of the gap. See Lawrence Mishel and Josh Bivens, "Identifying the Policy Levers Generating Wage Suppression and Wage Inequality," Economic Policy Institute Report, May 13, 2021, www.epi.org/unequalpower/publications/wage-suppression-inequality/.

[49] See Lazonick, "Profits Without Prosperity"; Lazonick, "Stock Buybacks"; Lenore Palladino, "The $1 Trillion Question: New Approaches to Regulating Stock Buybacks," *Yale Journal of Regulation*, 36, 2018: 89–105, https://papers.ssrn.com/sol3/papers.cfm?abstract_id=3274357; Lazonick and Jacobson, "Letter to SEC"; Lenore Palladino and William Lazonick, "Regulating Stock Buybacks: The $6.3 Trillion Question," *International Review of Applied Economics*, September 26, 2022, www.tandfonline.com/doi/full/10.1080/02692171.2022.2123459.

[50] Lazonick and Shin, *Predatory Value Extraction*.

shifted, often dramatically, the distribution of income within the business corporation from employees to shareholders.

Fundamental to this reversal was the capture of the SEC by free-market Chicago-School economists in 1981, following Ronald Reagan's election as president of the United States. Reagan's appointment of E. F. Hutton executive John Shad as SEC chair put the agency that was supposed to eliminate fraud and manipulation from the nation's financial markets under the leadership of a Wall Street banker for the first time since Joseph Kennedy was the inaugural holder of that position in 1934–1935.

In the second year of Shad's chairmanship, the SEC promulgated Rule 10b-18, which gives a company a safe harbor against manipulation charges in doing open-market repurchases.[51] Rule 10b-18 states that a company will not be charged with stock-price manipulation if, among other things, its buybacks on any single day are no more than 25 percent of the previous four weeks' average daily trading volume (ADTV). Under Rule 10b-18, moreover, there is no presumption of manipulation if the corporation's repurchases exceed the 25 percent ADTV limit.[52] Its adoption in 1982 was called a "regulatory about-face" from previous SEC views on the detection and prevention of manipulation of a company's stock price through open-market repurchases.[53] Under Rule 10b-18, many large publicly listed companies can do hundreds of millions of dollars of open-market repurchases per day, trading day after trading day, for the sole purpose of giving manipulative boosts to their stock prices (see Table 4).

Research undertaken by the Academic-Industry Research Network, supported by the Institute for New Economic Thinking, has analyzed the damage wrought by buybacks done by many of the companies listed in Table 4, which shows the top twenty repurchasers among industrial (or nonfinancial) corporations for 2010–2019.[54] Of these twenty companies, thirteen distributed more

---

[51] US Securities and Exchange Commission, "Purchases of Certain Equity Securities by the Issuer and Others; Adoption of Safe Harbor," November 17, 1982, *Federal Register* 47, 228, November 26, 1982: 53333–53341. See Palladino, "The $1 Trillion Question."

[52] US Securities and Exchange Commission, "Division of Trading and Markets: Answers to Frequently Asked Questions Concerning Rule 10b-18 ('Safe Harbor' for Issuer Repurchases)," *SEC Division of Trading and Markets*, https://www.sec.gov/divisions/market reg/r10b18faq0504.htm. For the safe harbor to be in effect, Rule 10b-18 also requires that the company refrain from doing buybacks at the beginning and end of the trading day, and that it execute all the buybacks through one broker only.

[53] Lloyd H. Feller and Mary Chamberlin, "Issuer Repurchases," *Review of Securities Regulation*, 17, 1, 1984: 993–998.

[54] See the references in note 39 and the websites of the Institute for New Economic Thinking (www .ineteconomics.org/research/experts/wlazonick), Academic-Industry Research Network (https:// theairnet.org), and *Harvard Business Review* (https://hbr.org/search?term=william+lazonick). See also William Lazonick, "Where Did You Go, Vice President Joe?" Institute for New Economic Thinking, March 4, 2022, www.ineteconomics.org/perspectives/blog/where-did-you-go-vice-president-joe.

Table 4 Twenty largest stock repurchasers, 2010–2019, among US industrial corporations, their buybacks from April 2020 through June 2022, and their SEC Rule 10b-18 safe-harbor average daily trading volume (ADTV) value for repurchases on 10/21/19, 6/23/21, and 3/27/22

COMPANY	$BB RANK	2010–2019			April 2020 through June 2022			ADTV		
		BB, $b.	BB/ NI%	(BB+DV)/ NI%	BB, $b.	BB/ NI%	(DV+BB)/ NI%	October 21, 2019, $m.	June 23, 2021, $m.	March 27, 2022, $m.
APPLE	1	305.0	73	94	184.8	93	110	1,597	2,526	4,146
ORACLE	2	113.7	121	145	39.3	153	186	183	261	236
MICROSOFT	3	101.1	48	92	65.8	39	65	754	1,522	2,514
EXXON MOBIL	4	92.4	35	80	6.2	27	171	166	410	815
IBM	5	88.2	71	107	0.0	0	108	125	144	145
CISCO SYSTEMS	6	81.5	100	144	10.5	38	93	226	254	305
PFIZER	7	76.7	60	116	2.0	4	48	146	235	425
WALMART	8	70.2	50	91	16.3	54	100	141	259	299
INTEL	9	66.8	51	87	12.4	29	59	219	318	497
HOME DEPOT	10	64.4	93	137	18.7	53	97	188	299	368
JOHNSON & JOHNSON	11	62.1	49	110	7.5	19	81	267	280	356

PROCTER & GAMBLE	12	54.9	52	117	21.0	66	126	186	319	299
AMGEN	13	51.2	92	129	13.0	92	155	97	164	205
GENERAL ELECTRIC	14	50.3	135	314	0.3	−26	−105	94	197	139
QUALCOMM	15	49.4	119	178	6.1	30	64	116	241	408
DISNEY	16	47.8	61	85	0.0	0	0	231	341	341
MERCK	17	45.8	81	172	0.8	3	62	144	265	217
MCDONALD'S	18	45.8	87	145	3.3	25	90	159	149	260
BOEING	19	43.4	87	137	0.0	0	0	292	708	521
GILEAD SCIENCES	20	39.6	56	75	1.2	21	156	93	122	181

Notes: BB = stock buybacks; DV = cash dividends; NI = net income; ADTV = stock-market value of the average daily trading volume limit to secure the safe harbor against stock-price manipulation charges under SEC Rule 10b-18.

Sources: Company 10-K and 10-Q filings with the SEC; Yahoo Finance daily historical stock prices.

than 100 percent of net income to shareholders over the decade while the other seven distributed 75 percent or more.

Coming into the pandemic, eleven companies on the list – Apple, Oracle, Microsoft, Cisco, Walmart, Intel, Home Depot, Johnson & Johnson, Amgen, Qualcomm, and Gilead – were in dominate-and-distribute mode, using the profits from their still-dominant market positions primarily to support their stock prices; while seven – Exxon Mobil, IBM, Procter & Gamble, General Electric (GE), Merck, McDonald's, and Boeing – were in downsize-and-distribute mode, distributing corporate cash to shareholders as they downsized their labor forces. Pfizer had been in downsize-and-distribute mode through 2018, but, in 2019 began to eschew buybacks and augmented its labor force for the sake of investment in innovation. Although Pfizer had long been one of the most financialized companies, it entered the pandemic with a new orientation to retain-and-reinvest – and then reaped bonanzas from its collaboration with Germany-based BioNTech in the development, manufacture, and delivery of the mRNA Covid-19 vaccine and its internally developed Paxlovid antiviral pill. Also, Disney had pivoted to retain-and-reinvest in the years just prior to the pandemic.

Table 4 also shows the buybacks done by these twenty companies from April 2020 through June 2022, representing the core period of the SARS-CoV-2 pandemic. Apple, Oracle, Walmart, Home Depot, Procter & Gamble, and Amgen spent 54 percent or more of net income on buybacks during this period. For Microsoft, Cisco, Intel, and Qualcomm, this proportion was in the 29–39 percent range. These ten companies benefited from very strong demand for their products and high profits during the pandemic.

Notwithstanding a sharp downturn in stock prices in March 2020, when the World Health Organization declared the spread of SARS-CoV-2 a pandemic, the US stock markets boomed during this social crisis. The last three columns of Table 4 show the generous ADTV "limits" for the twenty largest repurchasers among industrial companies, 2010–2019, at three points in time: in October 2019, in advance of the pandemic; in June 2021, when the Delta variant of SARS-CoV-2 was dominant in the United States, and in March 2022, when the highly transmissible Omicron variant emerged as widespread, prolonging the pandemic.[55] Except for McDonald's, the ADTV values had all risen, in many cases substantially, by June 2021 compared with October 2019, reflecting combinations of higher stock prices and higher trading volumes. The move-ment of ADTV from June 2021 to March 2022 was more mixed; most

---

[55] David J. Sencer, "CDC Museum COVID-19 Timeline," *Centers for Disease Control and Prevention*, www.cdc.gov/museum/timeline/covid19.html.

noteworthy was the continued explosion of the value of daily repurchases that Apple and Microsoft could do while availing themselves of Rule 10b-18's safe harbor.

Of the seven companies that entered the pandemic in downside-and-distribute mode, the financial condition of IBM, GE, and Boeing deteriorated further during it, constraining their financial capacity to do buybacks and even to pay dividends. IBM was known through the 1980s for its commitment to "lifelong employment," but in the early 1990s, in the name of MSV, the company's resource-allocation regime transformed rapidly and dramatically to downsize-and-distribute.[56] GE's corporate financialization, which originated in the conglomerate movement of the 1960s and continued during the reigns of CEOs Jack Welch (1981–2001) and Jeffrey Immelt (2001–2017), was given a coup de grâce by the predatory attack launched by hedge-fund activist Nelson Peltz (of Trian Partners) from October 2015, leaving GE with no choice but to dramatically reduce buybacks from 2018 and dividends from 2019.[57] As for Boeing, which became highly financialized after its merger with McDonnell Douglas in 1997, the obsession of the company's senior executives with stock yields bears much of the blame for the crashes of its 737 MAX planes in October 2018 and March 2019. From January 2013 through March 2019 – up to the week before the second crash on March 10 – Boeing did $43.4 billion in buybacks, equal to 118 percent of net income over this period, on top of 43 percent of net income distributed as dividends.[58]

Exxon Mobil was also financially constrained from doing buybacks in the years prior to the pandemic. Since the mid-1980s, high profits from high oil prices have funded the company's stock buybacks, while its dividends have

---

[56] Lazonick, *Sustainable Prosperity*, pp. 83–89, 121–128; William Lazonick, "The Financialization of the U.S. Corporation: What Has Been Lost, and How It Can Be Regained," *Seattle University Law Review*, 36, 2, 2013: 866–868.

[57] Mary A. O'Sullivan, *Contests for Corporate Control: Corporate Governance and Economic Performance in the United States and Germany*, Oxford University Press, 2000, Chs. 3–5; Thomas Gryta and Ted Mann, *Lights Out: Pride, Delusion, and the Fall of General Electric*, HarperCollins, 2021; William Lazonick and Matt Hopkins, "General Electric in the Grip of Predatory Value Extractors," Academic-Industry Research Network unpublished note, April 4, 2021, as a contribution to Nick Juravich and Arthur C. Wheaton, "Building a Sustainable Future for General Electric in Schenectady, New York, and Lynn, Massachusetts," School of Industrial and Labor Relations, Cornell University, and Labor Resource Center, UMass Boston, November 2021, https://www.umb.edu/media/umassboston/content-assets/lili-boulanger/pdf/UMB.Cornell.GE.Report.pdf; David Gelles, *The Man Who Broke Capitalism: How Jack Welch Gutted the Heartland and Crushed the Soul of Corporate America—and How to Undo His Legacy*, Simon & Schuster, 2022.

[58] Lazonick and Sakinç, "Make Passengers Safer?"; Peter Robison, *Flying Blind: The 737 MAX Tragedy and the Fall of Boeing*, Knopf Doubleday, 2021.

perpetually increased, whether oil prices are high or low.[59] For the decade, 2005–2014, Exxon Mobil averaged $22.0 billion in buybacks annually – by far the highest of any company over that period (second highest was IBM with a $12.3 billion annual average) – representing 61 percent of Exxon Mobil's exceedingly high profits, reaped from high oil prices. As oil prices declined dramatically from mid-2014 to mid-2020, cash-strapped Exxon Mobil had to rein in its buybacks, which declined yearly from $4.0 billion in 2015 to $155 million in 2021.

The explosion of crude oil prices during the pandemic, from $23.65 in March 2020 to $116.96 in May 2022,[60] turned Exxon Mobil's loss of $22.4 billion in 2020 into a profit of $23.0 billion in 2021 and $43.0 billion in the first nine months of 2022. Aiding the inflation of Exxon Mobil's bottom line was the slashing of its labor force from 72,000 in 2020 to 63,000 in 2021. With rising oil prices giving Exxon Mobil soaring profits during the first nine months of 2022, this company reverted to financialized form by gifting shareholders $11.4 billion in dividends and sharesellers $10.1 billion in buybacks.

Three companies – Disney, Pfizer, and Intel – explicitly abandoned buybacks before or during the pandemic for the sake of investing in the productive capabilities of their companies. Disney had decided to cancel its stock-repurchase program in August 2018 in anticipation of the heavy debt load that it would assume when it acquired Twenty-First Century Fox.[61] The company did no buybacks in the fourth quarter of fiscal 2018 (ended September 29). The acquisition was completed in March 2019, and Disney's revenues rose substantially in the second half of that fiscal year, while its profits declined. Disney's buyback program remained in suspension as the company entered the pandemic. With $2.9 billion in losses in 2020, Disney almost halved its previous dividend in fiscal 2020 by paying no dividends in the second half of fiscal year (ended October 3, 2020). Indeed, from April 2020 through September 2022, Disney distributed no corporate cash to shareholders, even though its revenues soared and profits recovered in 2022. Disney had cut employment from 223,000 at the end of fiscal 2019 to 190,000 at the end of fiscal 2021, but then, with its revenues rising from $67.4 billion in 2021 to $87.7 billion in 2022, increased its year-end labor force to 220,000.

A highly financialized corporation from the late 1980s, Pfizer committed to doing $8.9 billion in buybacks in early 2019, to be completed by August 1 of

[59] See Lazonick and Hopkins, "How 'Maximizing Shareholder Value' Minimized the Strategic National Stockpile," pp. 38–41.
[60] "Crude Oil Prices – 70 Year Historical Chart," Macrotrends, www.macrotrends.net/1369/crude-oil-price-history-chart.
[61] Emily Bary, "Disney Buybacks May Be in Pause until 2023, Citi Says," *MarketWatch*, April 21, 2020, www.marketwatch.com/story/disney-buybacks-may-be-on-pause-until-2023-citi-says-2020-04-21.

that year.[62] After this buybacks binge, however, the company ceased doing buybacks as it turned its strategic attention to conserving a portion of its profits to finance investment in its drug pipeline. Previously, Pfizer's strategy had been to acquire other companies with lucrative drugs on the market that had years of patent life left and to extract the profits from these drugs to fund its distributions to shareholders. By the late 2010s, however, with Big Pharma acquisition targets unavailable and the patents on a number of Pfizer's major drugs expiring, the board recognized that Pfizer itself could be taken over by another Big Pharma company unless it could develop high-revenue drugs internally.

For the sake of internal drug development, Pfizer refrained from doing buybacks from August 2019 through February 2022. Indeed, in an unusual move among US corporations, in January 2020 Pfizer publicly announced its commitment to forego buybacks that year, and it did so again in January 2021. The company did, however, increase its dividend in 2019, 2020, 2021, and the first nine months of 2022, paying out 48 percent of its substantial net income as dividends during the pandemic period, as defined in Table 4.

The implementation of this change in Pfizer's investment strategy followed the end of Ian Read's tenure as Pfizer CEO as of January 1, 2019, in favor of current CEO Albert Bourla. As CEO from 2011, Read had engaged in downsize-and-distribute.[63] In an earnings call with stock-market analysts in January 2020, Bourla made an extraordinary admission of the company's financialized past, declaring that Pfizer had stopped doing buybacks so that the company could invest in innovation:

> The reason why in our capital allocation, we are allocating right now money [is] to increase the dividend and also to invest in our business … all the CapEx to modernize our facilities. The reason why we don't do right now share repurchases, it is because we want to make sure that we maintain very

---

[62] Pfizer's broker executed $2.1 billion in open-market repurchases in the first quarter of 2019 (ended March 31) but none thereafter. In addition, on February 7, 2019, Pfizer entered into a $6.8 billion "accelerated share repurchase" (ASR) agreement with Goldman Sachs. A device for stock-price manipulation, an ASR enables a company to reduce its shares outstanding by the full number of shares in the agreement on the date on which it signs the ASR contract. This arrangement gives an immediate, that is, "accelerated," boost to the company's earnings-per-share (EPS), without the company transgressing the ADTV limit under Rule 10b-18. The bank (in this case Goldman Sachs) borrows the shares specified in the ASR agreement from asset funds that are not seeking to sell the shares. Then, during the life of the ASR agreement, the bank purchases the company's shares on the stock market in smaller amounts at its discretion at various points in time and returns the borrowed shares to the asset funds. In the case of Pfizer's 2019 $6.8 billion ASR, Goldman Sachs completed it on August 1, 2019.

[63] William Lazonick, Öner Tulum, Matt Hopkins, Mustafa Erdem Sakinç, and Ken Jacobson, "Financialization of the U.S. Pharmaceutical Industry," *Institute for New Economic Thinking*, December 2, 2019, https://www.ineteconomics.org/perspectives/blog/financialization-us-pharma-industry.

strong firepower to invest in the business. The past was a very different Pfizer. The past of the last decade had to deal with declining of revenues, constant declining of revenues. And we had to do what we had to do even if that was financial engineering, purchasing back ourselves. We couldn't invest them and create higher value. Now it's a very different situation. We are a very different company.[64]

Bourla did not explain why the "old" Pfizer – which, less than twelve months before, had done $8.9 billion in buybacks – "had to do what we had to do even if that was financial engineering, purchasing back ourselves." But his rambling statement to the analysts is a very rare recognition by a CEO of a major US corporation that stock buybacks are the enemy of investment in innovation.

Shortly thereafter, SARS-CoV-2 was declared a pandemic, and Pfizer found itself in what turned out to be a very lucrative partnership with BioNTech to develop, manufacture, and deliver the Covid-19 mRNA vaccine. Even though Pfizer's revenues almost doubled from $41.9 billion in 2020 to $81.3 billion in 2021, with profits soaring from $9.6 billion to $22.0 billion, the company refrained from doing buybacks, while the dividend payout ratio declined from 88 percent to 40 percent. With revenues and profits continuing to explode in the first nine months of 2022, bolstered by sales of Paxlovid (given emergency use authorization by the Food and Drug Administration in December 2021), Pfizer did $2.0 billion in buybacks, all of them in March. We can assume that Pfizer timed these repurchases to give a manipulative boost to its sagging stock price.[65] If so, it apparently worked; on March 1, Pfizer's stock price had sunk to $45.75 but was then pumped up to $55.17 on April 8. With the release of its results for the second quarter of 2022, however, Pfizer stated that the company "does not anticipate any additional share repurchases in 2022."[66] Pfizer's self-restraint may be based in its senior executives' recognition that Pfizer's windfall profits from its Covid-19 medicines are unlikely to last.[67]

As the case of Pfizer clearly illustrates, even within a business corporation that has become a leading repurchaser of its own stock, there is an ongoing

---

[64] Pfizer Inc., "Event Brief of Q4 2019 Pfizer Inc Earnings Call – Final," *CQ FD Disclosure*, January 28, 2020.

[65] In Pfizer Inc., "Pfizer Reports First-Quarter 2022 Results," *Pfizer Press Release*, May 3, 2022, p. 2. Under "Capital Allocation," the report states that a $3.3-billion repurchase authorization remains, but that "[c]urrent financial guidance does not anticipate any additional share repurchases in 2022." https://s28.q4cdn.com/781576035/files/doc_financials/2022/q1/Q1-2022-PFE-Earnings-Release.pdf.

[66] Pfizer Inc., "Pfizer's Second Quarter Sees Historical Sales and Bold Goals," *Pfizer Investor Insights*, July 28, 2022, https://insights.pfizer.com/second-quarter-results/.

[67] Jonathan Weber, "Is Pfizer Stock a Buy after Strong Earnings? Massive Profits Won't Last," *Seeking Alpha,* August 4, 2022, https://seekingalpha.com/article/4529640-is-pfizer-stock-buy-after-strong-earnings.

tension between innovation and financialization, with specific sets of circumstances determining the outcome.[68] Intel, No. 9 in buybacks in Table 4, offers another example of a shift in corporate strategy, entailing cessation of buybacks, from financialization to innovation in an advanced-technology industry.

Once the world leader in chip fabrication, a financialized Intel found itself falling behind in the face of innovative global competition. Under new leadership, however, Intel is now seeking to invest in advanced nanometer fabrication facilities with the goal of catching up with industry frontrunners TSMC and Samsung Electronics.[69] Intel ceased doing stock buybacks from the second quarter of 2021 after replacing CEO Robert Swan, a finance expert, with Pat Gelsinger, a technology expert.[70] In a *60 Minutes* interview, Gelsinger said that a condition of his taking the top Intel job was assurance from the company's board that Intel would "not be anywhere near as focused on buybacks going forward as we have in the past."[71]

In a subsequent interview with *CNET* in November 2021, Gelsinger was much more expansive and emphatic.[72] He recounted how, before taking the CEO job, he had written a strategy paper for Intel's board, for which he got their unanimous agreement. "I was concerned," Gelsinger said in the interview, "about how we get the process roadmap back in shape." He continued:

> We underinvested in capital. I went to the board and said: "We're done with buybacks. We are investing in factories." And that is going to be the use of our cash as we go forward. And they aggressively supported that perspective; that we needed to just start investing, and those investments would start creating a cycle of momentum that would get our factory teams executing better.

During 2022, Gelsinger was in the forefront of lobbying for the CHIPS and Science Act, signed into law on August 9, 2022. The Act provides $52.7 billion in federal government subsidies to semiconductor companies operating in the United States for research development, manufacturing, and workforce

[68] See Öner Tulum, Antonio Andreoni, and William Lazonick, *From Financialisation to Innovation in UK Big Pharma: AstraZeneca and GlaxoSmithKline*, Cambridge Elements in Reinventing Capitalism, Cambridge University Press, 2022, https://www.cambridge.org/core/elements/from-financialisation-to-innovation-in-uk-big-pharma/A077D6158F0A945ED53F3F125EE0650F.
[69] William Lazonick and Matt Hopkins, "How Intel Financialized and Lost Leadership in Semiconductor Fabrication," *Institute for New Economic Thinking*, July 7, 2021, https://www.ineteconomics.org/perspectives/blog/how-intel-financialized-and-lost-leadership-in-semiconductor-fabrication.
[70] Lazonick and Hopkins, "Why the CHIPS Are Down."
[71] Lesley Stahl, "Chip Shortage Highlights U.S. Dependence on Fragile Supply Chain," *60 Minutes*, May 2, 2021, www.cbsnews.com/news/semiconductor-chip-shortage-60-minutes-2021-05-02/.
[72] CNET, "Intel CEO Pat Gelsinger! (CNET's Full Interview)," *CNET Highlights*, November 19, 2021, www.youtube.com/watch?v=_y-GWcsK6Ag&t=5s.

development.[73] Through the first nine months of 2022, Intel refrained from doing buybacks. For its part, the Biden administration has stated that the distribution of the funds under the Act "come with strong guardrails" including "preventing companies from using taxpayer funds for stock buybacks and shareholder dividends."[74] For the time being, Intel has erected its own guardrail by eschewing buybacks, but it remains to be seen whether, in meting out CHIPS subsidies, the US government will regulate distributions to shareholders by corporate recipients.[75]

A key point of this overview of the payouts to shareholders of the largest repurchasers is that individual companies make decisions concerning their level of buyback activity, and hence an analysis of the relation between stock buybacks and corporate performance must examine particular corporate trajectories, including changes in strategic control. The theory of innovative enterprise provides an analytical framework for conducting this company-level research while recognizing the importance of the institutional and industrial contexts within which a particular corporation operates.

By the same token, analyses done at the industrial-sector level can be misleading because of, at times, large variation in distributions to shareholders among companies within the same sector. In semiconductors, for example, while Intel has been paying substantial dividends and was among the largest repurchasers in the United States for the last two decades, its rival Advanced Micro Devices (AMD) has never paid a dividend in its fifty-three-year history, and prior to 2020, the only open-market repurchases that it had done amounted to $77 million in 2001, after its board authorized a $300-million repurchase program. Given Intel's large-scale distributions to shareholders from the late 1990s, if one were to take average dividends and buybacks of Intel and AMD in the 2000s and 2010s as indicative of payouts in the US semiconductor industry, one would know nothing about the actual distribution policies of either company.

---

[73] White House, "FACT SHEET: CHIPS and Science Act Will Lower Costs, Create Jobs, Strengthen Supply Chains, and Counter China," *Briefing Room Press Release*, August 9, 2022, https://www.whitehouse.gov/briefing-room/statements-releases/2022/08/09/fact-sheet-chips-and-science-act-will-lower-costs-create-jobs-strengthen-supply-chains-and-counter-china/.

[74] Ibid. See also US Department of Commerce, "Commerce Department Launches CHIPS.gov for CHIPS Program," *DOC Press Release*, August 25, 2022, https://www.commerce.gov/news/press-releases/2022/08/commerce-department-launches-chipsgov-chips-program-implementation; Ana Swanson, "Biden Administration Releases Plan for $50 Billion Investment in Chips," *New York Times*, September 6, 2022, https://www.nytimes.com/2022/09/06/business/economy/biden-tech-chips.html.

[75] For a call to implement these guardrails subsequent to the passage of the CHIPS and Science Act, see Sen. Elizabeth Warren and Sen. Tammy Baldwin and Reps. Sean Casten, Jamaal Bowman, Pramila Jayapal, and Bill Foster, "Letter to Commerce Secretary Gina Raimondo," October 4, 2022, https://www.warren.senate.gov/imo/media/doc/2022.10.04%20Letter%20to%20Commerce%20re%20CHIPS%20Stock%20Buybacks.pdf.

Moreover, in 2021, just as Intel refrained from doing buybacks, AMD became devoted to them. In 2020, AMD did $78 billion in buybacks to cover employee withholding taxes on vesting of employee equity grants. On May 19, 2021, however, with its profits during the pandemic at about seven times its profits in each of 2018 and 2019 (which were good years for the company), AMD announced a $4-billion repurchase program.[76] Then, for the sole purpose of giving manipulative boosts to its stock price, AMD did $256 million in buybacks under its new program in the second quarter of 2021, another $748 million in the third quarter, and $758 million in the fourth quarter. In February 2022, the AMD board authorized an additional $8 billion in buybacks,[77] and in the first nine months of 2022, still paying no dividends, AMD did $3.5 billion in open-market repurchases, 2.7 times its net income during this period.

While stock prices can increase because of innovation and speculation, increasing numbers of companies, within and across industries, compete in stock-price performance by manipulation via buybacks.[78] In the history of predatory value extraction, no company has set the manipulation bar as high as Apple, No. 1 in Table 4, whose buybacks over 2010–2019 were triple those of Oracle as No. 2 and Microsoft as No. 3. As shown in Table 4, Apple's extraordinarily high ADTV "limit" of $1.6 billion per trading day in October 2019 exploded to $2.5 billion in June 2021 and $4.1 billion in March 2022 during the pandemic. From October 2012 through September 2022, Apple threw away $553 billion – 93 percent of its enormous net income – on open-market repurchases, the sole purpose of which was to manipulate the company's stock price. In addition, Apple funneled $129 billion in dividends to shareholders, absorbing another 22 percent of net income.

Apple calls these distributions to shareholders its "Capital Return Program."[79] But how can Apple "return" cash to those who have never given the company anything? The only money that Apple has raised from the public stock market in its forty-six-year history was the $97 million realized from its

---

[76] Advanced Micro Devices, "AMD Announces $4 Billion Share Repurchase Program," *AMD Press Release*, May 19, 2021, https://ir.amd.com/news-events/press-releases/detail/1001/amd-announces-4-billion-share-repurchase-program.

[77] Advanced Micro Devices, "AMD Announces New $8 Billion Share Repurchase Authorization," *AMD Press Release*, February 24, 2022, www.amd.com/en/press-releases/2022-02-24-amd-announces-new-8-billion-share-repurchase-authorization.

[78] William Lazonick, "The Functions of the Stock Market and the Fallacies of Shareholder Value," in Ciaran Driver and Grahame Thompson, eds., *What Next for Corporate Governance?* Oxford University Press, 2018: 117–151.

[79] William Lazonick, "Apple's 'Capital Return' Program: Where Are the Patient Capitalists?" *Institute for New Economic Thinking*, November 13, 2018, https://www.ineteconomics.org/perspectives/blog/apples-capital-return-program-where-are-the-patient-capitalists.

initial public offering (IPO) in 1980.[80] When, in the summer of 2013, corporate predator Carl Icahn purchased $3.6 billion worth of Apple shares on NASDAQ and then, in the winter of 2016, sold that stake on NASDAQ for a $2-billion gain, shares outstanding on the stock market simply passed from one stock trader to another.

Not one cent of the $3.6 billion that Icahn spent on acquiring these outstanding shares went to Apple. It would be ludicrous, therefore, to call Icahn an "investor" in Apple as a value-creating company. To the contrary, apparently succumbing to Icahn's wealth, visibility, hype, and influence, Apple CEO Tim Cook and his board of directors helped the hedge-fund activist reap those financial gains by doing $45.0 billion in buybacks in fiscal 2014 (ended September 27) and $35.3 billion in fiscal 2015 – the first and third largest annual expenditures on buybacks ever executed by any company at that time (Exxon Mobil's buybacks in 2008 were $35.7 billion).[81]

Then, in the winter of 2016, as Icahn was dumping his Apple shares, Warren Buffett, using Berkshire Hathaway money, started buying Apple shares on NASDAQ until by September 2018 he had shelled out $36.3 billion, giving him 5.1 percent of Apple's shares outstanding. In May 2018, Buffett enthused in an interview: "I'm delighted to see [Apple] repurchasing shares. I love the idea of having our 5 percent, or whatever it is, maybe grow to 6 or 7 percent without our laying out a dime."[82] After having repurchased $32.9 billion in 2017, Apple granted Buffett his wish, as the company's buybacks were $72.7 billion in 2018, $66.9 billion in 2019, $72.4 billion in 2020, $86.0 billion in 2021, and $89.4 billion in 2022 (fiscal year ended September 24).

By January 2022, Buffett's Apple shares were valued at $160 billion, even after he had sold 12 percent of his original stake for $13 billion and had raked in another $3 billion in dividends.[83] He now held almost 5.6 percent of Apple's stock outstanding, a figure that would have been 6.3 percent if Buffett had not sold some of his shares. While Buffett was remarkably candid in saying that he

[80] William Lazonick, "Numbers Show Apple Shareholders Have Already Gotten Plenty," *Harvard Business Review*, October 16, 2014, https://hbr.org/2014/10/numbers-show-apple-shareholders-have-already-gotten-plenty.

[81] William Lazonick, Matt Hopkins, and Ken Jacobson, "What We Learn about Inequality from Carl Icahn's $2 Billion 'No Brainer'," *Institute for New Economic Thinking*, June 6, 2016, https://www.ineteconomics.org/perspectives/blog/what-we-learn-about-inequality-from-carl-icahns-2-billion-apple-no-brainer.

[82] Trevor Hunnicutt and Jonathan Stempel, "Warren Buffett Is Now Apple's Biggest Shareholder—and He Wants to Own More," *Financial Post,* May 17, 2018, https://financialpost.com/investing/rpt-wrapup-3-buffett-craves-more-apple-shares-endorses-its-buybacks.

[83] CNBCTV18.com, "Warren Buffett's Stake in Apple Makes Over $120 Billion This Week," *CNBCTV,* January 5, 2022, https://www.cnbctv18.com/business/warren-buffetts-stake-in-apple-makes-over-120-billion-this-week-12020572.htm.

could increase his percentage of Apple's outstanding shares "without our laying out a dime," he might have added that not one cent of the $36.3 billion that he paid to buy Apple's shares on the market flowed into the company to invest in its productive capabilities or for any other purpose.

With the help of $433 billion in Apple buybacks since the winter of 2016, when Buffett began accumulating the company's stock, through fiscal 2022, Berkshire Hathaway has profited immensely from the greatest treasury robbery in US corporate history. The looting has, as far as we know, been perfectly legal because of SEC Rule 10b-18, adopted without public comment on November 17, 1982 – the real birth date, in historical retrospect, of the pernicious and flawed ideology that, for the sake of economic efficiency, a business corporation should be run to "maximize shareholder value."[84]

This is not the first time that Apple's top management has been guided by MSV as its corporate goal. In 1985, after founder Steve Jobs was ousted from the company, Apple CEO John Scully sought to drive up the company's stock yield, and his own pay, with dividends and buybacks. By 1996 and 1997, Apple was taking huge losses and, to avert bankruptcy, had to be bailed out by Microsoft in the form of a $150-million purchase of preferred shares.[85] It was in this context that Jobs regained strategic control of Apple and reinstituted a retain-and-reinvest regime – eschewing distributions to shareholders in order to reinvest profits in Apple's productive capabilities – culminating in the launch of the iPhone in 2007.

Jobs passed away in October 2011. During his tenure as Apple CEO from September 1997 to August 2011, the company's share price had risen by 7,000 percent. Innovation had amply rewarded loyal Apple shareholders, in part because Jobs invested in productive capabilities instead of doing buybacks to manipulate the company's stock price. Tim Cook, Jobs' successor as CEO, had previously been Apple's chief supply-chain executive, with his most profound contribution to the company having been outsourcing its manufacturing to Foxconn in China. In the fourth quarter of fiscal 2012, Apple paid dividends for the first time since 1996, and, in the first quarter of fiscal 2013, the current buybacks spree commenced.

In October 2014, as shareholder Icahn was pressuring CEO Cook to do $100 billion in buybacks, I wrote an article questioning Apple's so-called Capital Return Program, which had been stepped up in April 2014 when the Apple board had authorized a total of $90 billion in buybacks and $40 billion in

---

[84] Lazonick, "Is the Most Unproductive Firm."
[85] William Lazonick, Mariana Mazzucato, and Öner Tulum, "Apple's Changing Business Model: What Should the World's Richest Company Do with All Those Profits?" *Accounting Forum*, 37, 4, 2013: 249–267.

dividends by December 2015.[86] I also published an open letter to CEO Cook, suggesting ways in which, instead of doing buybacks, he could allocate Apple's cash to innovative investments and support an equitable income distribution, including (a) more compensation for tens of thousands of employees in Apple stores (not to mention hundreds of thousands of people working at companies in Apple's global supply chain); (b) more educational support to enhance the career opportunities for Apple employees, especially for those in dead-end jobs in Apple stores and call centers; (c) collaboration with government agencies in social investments in knowledge and infrastructure; and (d) collaboration with government agencies in social innovation to develop the technologies of the future to meet society's needs.[87]

In October 2021, Matt Hopkins and I published an INET working paper, "Why the CHIPS Are Down,"[88] in which we ask why the US federal government should provide the US semiconductor industry with $52 billion in subsidies under the CHIPS for America Act (subsequently passed into law as the CHIPS and Science Act),[89] when the tech companies, including Apple, that were lobbying for its passage[90] did about seventeen times the requested subsidy in buybacks in 2011–2020. We also note that Apple's decisions to outsource the fabrication of its iPhone chips, first to Samsung Electronics and then, from 2015, exclusively to Taiwan Semiconductor Manufacturing Company (TSMC), have aided these two companies in their emergence as the world's leading chip foundries.

In 2010, a prominent electronics-industry journalist, Mark LaPedus, penned an article entitled "Apple should build a fab," addressed to Apple CEO Jobs.[91] At the time, Apple was reliant for chip fabrication on its emerging smartphone competitor, Samsung Electronics. LaPedus recognized that "in an age when real

---

[86] Lazonick, "Numbers Show Apple Shareholders."

[87] William Lazonick, "What Apple Should Do with Its Massive Piles of Money," *Harvard Business Review*, October 20, 2014, https://hbr.org/2014/10/what-apple-should-do-with-its-massive-piles-of-money.

[88] Lazonick and Hopkins, "Why the CHIPS Are Down."

[89] Sherrod Brown, "Brown, Portman Urge Congressional Leadership to Revise and Swiftly Pass Legislation to Invest in Manufacturing and Address Global Semiconductor Shortage," *Sherrod Brown Press Release*, January 7, 2022, https://www.brown.senate.gov/newsroom/press/release/brown-portman-pass-manufacturing-semiconductor-shortage.

[90] Semiconductor Industry Association "SIA calls for House passage of legislation to advance U.S. technology leadership," SIA, June 28, 2021, www.semiconductors.org/sia-calls-for-house-passage-of-legislation-to-advance-u-s-technology-leadership/; Semiconductor Industry Association, "SIA Members: Working together to advance the U.S. semiconductor industry," https://www.semiconductors.org/about/members/, Semiconductors in America Coalition, "Letter: SIAC calls on congressional leaders to fund CHIPS Act," SIAC, July 28, 2021, www.chipsinamerica.org.

[91] Mark LaPedus, "Apple Should Build a Fab," *EDN*, August 26, 2010, www.edn.com/apple-should-build-a-fab/.

men go fabless, I concede it's an unconventional idea. You might think it's absurd. But an Apple A4 fab today could keep the iProduct franchise in hay – and Samsung at bay."

But in August 2011 Jobs passed the CEO torch to Cook, and Apple investing in its own fab was a road not taken. In 2021, under pressure from US trade negotiators, Samsung and TSMC began building new state-of-the-art fabs in the United States, at a projected cost of $17 billion and $12 billion, respectively.[92] In comparison, the $86 billion that Apple spent on buybacks in fiscal 2021 alone was three times the combined US fab investments of Samsung and TSMC announced in that year.

When, in May 2018, Cook was asked what he planned to do with the $285 billion in cash that the company was repatriating from abroad as a result of tax breaks provided by the Republican Tax Cuts and Jobs Act of 2017, he replied:

> We're going to create a new site, a new campus within the United States. We're going to hire 20,000 people. We're going to spend $30 billion in capital expenditure over the next several years. Number one, we're investing, and investing a ton, in this country. We're also going to buy some of our stock, as we view our stock as a good value.[93]

The buybacks that Cook called "some of our stock" amounted to $73 billion in 2018 (122 percent of net income), far surpassing Apple's previous high of $45 billion in 2014, which had been carried out at the behest of Carl Icahn. As it turned out, 2018 was the beginning of a five-year buyback binge that totaled $387 billion (106 percent of net income), to the delight of Warren "without our laying out a dime" Buffett. Certainly, we can ask CEO Cook: "Good value" for whom?

Apple's board authorizes the company's massive buybacks. The Apple director with the longest tenure is Arthur D. Levinson, who has been on the board since 2000 and its chair since late 2011. Levinson is a scientist who spent most of his career with the pioneering biopharmaceutical company Genentech, joining the firm in 1980 and serving as its CEO from 1995 to 2009 and as

---

[92] Anton Shilov, "Texas to Get Multiple New Fabs as Samsung and TI to Spend $47 Billion on New Facilities," *AnandTech,* November 24, 2021, www.anandtech.com/show/17086/texas-to-get-multiple-new-fabs-as-samsung-and-ti-to-spend-47-billion-on-new-facilities; Katie Tarasov, "Inside TSMC, the Taiwanese Chipmaking Giant That's Building a New Plant in Phoenix," *CNBC,* October 16, 2021, www.cnbc.com/2021/10/16/tsmc-taiwanese-chipmaker-ramping-production-to-end-chip-shortage.html.

[93] WRAL TechWire, "Apple CEO Confirms Commitment to Build New Campus, Hire 20,000 New Employees," *WRAL,* June 15, 2018, https://wraltechwire.com/2018/06/15/apple-ceo-reaffirms-commitment-to-build-new-campus-hire-20000-new-employees/.

chairman of its board from 1999 to 2014.[94] Since 2013, he has been the CEO of Calico Life Sciences LLC, the privately held venture of Alphabet. From 1990, Levinson and other Genentech employees were protected from the pressures of predatory value extractors by the majority ownership of the company by F. Hoffmann-La Roche AG, a Switzerland-based corporation better known simply as Roche, that has been both the least financialized and most innovative of the global Big Pharma companies.[95] Calico's parent, Alphabet, keeps corporate predators at bay by means of its treble-class (A, B, C) share structure.[96] Given his own employment experience, at Genentech and Calico, Dr. Levinson could have advised Apple on how it might have invested a portion of the hundreds of billions of dollars that it has wasted on buybacks in supporting companies engaged in medicine innovation.

The Apple director with the second-longest tenure is Albert Arnold Gore Jr., who has been on its board since 2003. The former US vice president and Democratic candidate for president in 2000 has been one of the world's leading activists for social awareness of the threat of global warming to human existence. In 2006, Gore released his documentary on climate change, *An Inconvenient Truth*, which went on to win an Oscar.[97] But what about the inconvenient truth of the looting of Apple's corporate treasury under his watch? Mr. Gore could have advised Apple on how it might have invested even a portion of the hundreds of billions of dollars that it has wasted on buybacks to combat climate change.

Have Cook, Levinson, and Gore so thoroughly imbibed MSV ideology that they believe that Apple is actually "returning" corporate cash to people who just buy and sell shares outstanding on the stock market? Or are they so frightened by the possibility that they might lose their positions of strategic control at Apple to hedge-fund activists that they appease them with hundreds of billions of dollars in buybacks? Their responses are, of course, most welcome.

---

[94] Wikipedia, "Arthur D. Levinson," *Wikipedia,* https://en.wikipedia.org/wiki/Arthur_D._Levinson.

[95] Tulum and Lazonick, "Financialized Corporations."

[96] Google was renamed Alphabet in 2015 when the company issued Class C nonvoting shares, publicly traded on NASDAQ, in addition to previously issued Class A voting shares, also publicly listed on NASDAQ, and Class B shares, with ten times the voting power of Class A shares, held primarily by Google founders Sergey Brin and Larry Page. Previously, Google's distributions of Class A shares to a broad base of its employees as stock-based compensation had eroded the majority voting power of Brin and Page. With Class A, B, and C shares, Google became a subsidiary of Alphabet. Henceforth, Alphabet issued publicly traded Class C nonvoting shares to employees in their compensation packages, enabling Brin and Page to maintain voting control of Alphabet.

[97] Steve Gorman, "Gore's 'Inconvenient Truth' Wins Documentary Oscar," *Reuters,* February 25, 2007, www.reuters.com/article/us-oscars-gore1/gores-inconvenient-truth-wins-documentary-oscar-idUSN2522150720070226.

Whatever the motives of Cook and his board in carrying out the largest looting of a corporate treasury in US history, academic cover for their actions as value-extracting insiders has come from a species of professional economists known as "agency theorists," whose rationale for distributing profits to shareholders in the form of not only dividends but also buybacks is that shareholders, and shareholders alone, make risky investments in the business corporation, without a guaranteed return, and hence only shareholders have a claim on profits if and when they occur.[98] The theory assumes that other stakeholders in the corporation, including workers, receive guaranteed prices (i.e., wages) for their productive contributions. Agency theory, however, overstates the risks borne by shareholders in making corporate investments, while ignoring risky investments in productive resources by not only workers but also taxpayers that can enable business corporations to generate revenues and profits.

The fact is that public shareholders do not, as a rule, invest directly in the firm. Rather, once a firm is publicly listed, households or asset managers become shareholders by purchasing shares outstanding on the stock market. In placing their funds in shares listed on a highly liquid stock market such as NYSE or NASDAQ, public shareholders take little risk; they enjoy limited liability if they hold the shares and, given the liquidity of the stock market, at any instant and at a very low transaction cost they can sell the shares at the going market price.

In other words, public shareholders are value extractors, not value creators. The generation of innovative products requires value-creating investment in productive capabilities, which are inherently illiquid, and hence the investment is risky. As we have seen, investments in innovation are uncertain, collective, and cumulative. An innovative enterprise requires strategic control to confront uncertainty, organizational integration to engage in collective learning, and financial commitment to sustain cumulative learning. When, as in the case of a start-up, financiers make equity investments in the absence of a liquid market for the company's shares, these early investors in the company's value-creating capabilities face the risk that the firm will not be able to generate a competitive product. Even then, however, their risk is mitigated by the existence of a highly liquid stock market on which the firm can do an IPO, permitting these financial investors to reap financial

[98] William Lazonick, "Innovative Enterprise Solves the Agency Problem: The Theory of the Firm, Financial Flows, and Economic Performance," Institute for New Economic Thinking Working Paper No. 62, August 28, 2017, www.ineteconomics.org/research/research-papers/innovative-enterprise-solves-the-agency-problem; Lazonick, "Maximizing Shareholder Value as an Ideology of Predatory Value Extraction."

returns, often before the company has generated a commercial product, let alone a profit.[99]

To make such a speculative and liquid market available to private-equity investors, NASDAQ was launched in 1971 by electronically linking the previously fragmented, and hence relatively illiquid, over-the-counter markets. NASDAQ became an inducement to direct investment in start-ups precisely because it offered the prospect of a quick IPO taking place within just a few years after a firm was founded. For that reason, venture capitalists can use a quotation on NASDAQ as an *exit strategy*. In effect, through an IPO, they can exit an illiquid, high-risk direct investment by turning it into a liquid, low-risk portfolio investment. After an IPO, if the former direct investors decide to hold on to their shares, they are in the same portfolio-investor position as any other public shareholder: They can use the stock market to buy and sell shares at low transaction cost whenever they choose to do so.

As private shareholders, venture capitalists bear the risk of making direct investments in productive resources, but from the 1970s, institutions evolved in the United States that could make that risk ephemeral by enabling them to transform their illiquid private equity holdings into liquid public shareholdings. In contrast, households as taxpayers, through government agencies, and as workers, through the business corporations that employ them, also bear risk in making investments in productive resources, but without the availability of financial markets for monetizing the productive assets in which they have invested. From this perspective, households as both taxpayers and workers invest in innovation and have valid economic claims on the distribution of profits, if and when profits occur.

Through government investments in human capabilities and physical infrastructure, taxpayers regularly provide productive resources to companies without a guaranteed return. As an important example, but only one of many, the 2022 budget of the US National Institutes of Health (NIH) was $45 billion, part of a total NIH investment in life-sciences research spanning 1938–2022 that adds up to almost $1.5 trillion in 2022 dollars.[100] Businesses that make use of NIH-sponsored research benefit from the public knowledge that it generates. As risk-bearers, taxpayers who fund investments in such research or in physical infrastructure such as roads, have a claim on resulting corporate profits, if and

---

[99] See William Lazonick and Öner Tulum, "US Biopharmaceutical Finance and the Sustainability of the Biotech Business Model," *Research Policy*, 40, 9, 2011: 1170–1187.

[100] National Institutes of Health, Office of Budget, "Appropriations History by Institute/Center (1938 to Present)," https://officeofbudget.od.nih.gov/approp_hist.html; National Institutes of Health, Office of Budget, "Supplementary Appropriation Data Table for History of Congressional Appropriations, Fiscal Years 2020–2022," https://officeofbudget.od.nih.gov/pdfs/FY22/Approp%20History%20by%20IC%20FY%202020%20-%20FY%202022.pdf.

when they are generated. Through the tax system, governments, representing households as taxpayers, seek to extract this return from corporations that make profitable use of government spending.

No matter what corporate tax rate prevails, however, households as taxpayers face the uncertainty that changes in technological, market, and/or competitive conditions may prevent enterprises from generating profits and the related business tax revenues that serve as a return on the taxpayers' investments in physical infrastructure and human capabilities. Moreover, tax rates are politically determined; households as taxpayers face the political uncertainty that predatory value extractors may convince government policymakers that they will not be able to make value-creating investments unless they are given tax cuts or financial subsidies that will permit adequate profits. Households as taxpayers face the risk that politicians may be put in power who accede to these demands for predatory value extraction.

Through their skills and efforts, workers regularly make productive contributions to the companies for which they work that are beyond the levels required to lay claim to their current pay. However, they do so without guaranteed returns.[101] Any employer who is seeking to generate a higher-quality, lower-cost product knows the profound difference in the productivity levels of those employees who just punch the clock to get their daily pay – what has recently become known as "quiet quitting" among white-collar workers[102] – and those who are committed to supporting the company's goals of generating products that can compete in terms of quality and cost. An innovative company wants workers who apply their skills and efforts to organizational learning so that they can make enduring productive contributions – including those that will enable the development of the firm's next generation of high-quality, low-cost products.

For their part, in making these productive contributions, employees expect that they will be able to build their careers within the company, putting themselves in positions to reap future benefits at work and in retirement. Yet these potential careers and returns are not guaranteed. In fact, under the downsize-and-distribute resource-allocation regime that MSV ideology legitimizes, these careers and returns are generally undermined.

Workers, therefore, supply their skills and efforts to the process of generating innovative products that, if successful, could create value, but they take the

---

[101] Lazonick, *Competitive Advantage*; Lazonick, "The Theory of Innovative Enterprise."

[102] Alyson Krueger, "Who Is Quiet Quitting For?" *New York Times*, August 23, 2022, https://www.nytimes.com/2022/08/23/style/quiet-quitting-tiktok.html; Greg Rosalsky and Alina Selyukh, "The Economics Behind 'Quiet Quitting'—and What We Should Call It Instead," *NPR*, September 13, 2022, www.npr.org/sections/money/2022/09/13/1122059402/the-economics-behind-quiet-quitting-and-what-we-should-call-it-instead.

risk that their endeavors could be in vain. Far from reaping expected gains in the form of higher remuneration, more job security, and better working conditions, employees could face cuts in pay and benefits, or even find themselves laid off. Even if the innovation process is successful, workers face the possibility that the institutional environment in which MSV prevails will empower corporate executives to cut some workers' wages and lay off other workers – all so that the value they helped to create can be redirected to shareholders, including the senior executives themselves with their copious stock-based pay as well as hedge-fund managers whose stock-trading strategies count buybacks as money in the bank.[103] In short, the corporate resource-allocation strategy may transform from retain-and-reinvest to downsize-and-distribute, with devastating impacts on the realized gains that committed employees had expected and deserved.

As risk-bearers, therefore, taxpayers whose money supports business corporations and workers whose efforts generate productivity improvements have claims on corporate profits, if and when they occur. MSV ignores the risk-reward relation for households as both taxpayers and workers in the operation and performance of business corporations.[104] MSV implies that public shareholders derive their gains by extracting value as a reward for taking the risk of contributing to processes that create value. Thus, as we have seen, when corporations pay dividends or do buybacks, MSV mischaracterizes these distributions as "returning" capital to shareholders. The irony of MSV is that public shareholders – whom agency theory deems to be the firm's sole risk-bearers – typically never invest in the value-creating capabilities of the company at all. Rather, they purchase outstanding corporate equities on the stock market with the expectation that dividend income will be forthcoming while they hold the shares and that the stock price will have risen to yield a financial gain when they decide to sell the shares.

Proponents of MSV may accept that a company needs to retain some cash flow to maintain the functioning of its physical capital, but they generally view labor as an interchangeable commodity that can be hired and fired as needed on the labor market. In addition, they typically ignore the contributions that households as taxpayers make to business value creation. Rooted in the neoclassical theory of the market economy, MSV assumes that markets, not organizations, allocate resources to their most efficient uses. But lacking a theory of

---

[103] Lazonick and Shin, *Predatory Value Extraction*.

[104] Lazonick, "The Financialization of the U.S. Corporation"; William Lazonick and Mariana Mazzucato, "The Risk-Reward Nexus in the Innovation-Inequality Relationship," *Industrial and Corporate Change*, 22, 4, 2013: 1093–1128; Lazonick, "Maximizing Shareholder Value as an Ideology of Predatory Value Extraction."

innovative enterprise, agency theory cannot explain how the "most efficient uses" are created and transformed over time.[105]

It is the triad of government agencies, household units, and business corporations that invests in the productive capabilities that underpin economic growth. These investments determine both the "most efficient" uses at a given point in time and the extent to which these "most efficient" uses become more productive over time.[106] Product markets, labor markets, and financial markets are outcomes, not causes, of this productivity growth.[107]

The MSV slogan is "disgorge the free cash flow."[108] Once we debunk the shareholder-value myth, the massive buybacks since the mid-1980s raise a significant question: How much of the cash flow that both shareholders and managers have deemed to be "free" has been misappropriation of funds that should have gone to households as taxpayers and households as workers as returns on the money and effort their members invested in the productive capabilities that generated corporate revenues and profits?[109]

For about three decades after World War II, income distribution became somewhat more equal, and a middle class of both high-school-educated blue-collar workers and college-educated white-collar workers thrived. In contrast, over the past four to five decades, the United States has experienced extreme concentration of income among the richest households and the erosion of middle-class employment opportunities for most of the population.[110] These two economic problems have been integrally related as business corporations have shifted from retain-and-reinvest to downsize-and-distribute, legitimized by the ideology that companies should be governed to maximize shareholder value.[111]

5 Reforming Corporate Governance for Sustainable Prosperity

With the election of Joseph R. Biden Jr. as president of the United States, Americans got a leader whose stated objective as a candidate was to put the nation back on a path to stable and equitable growth.[112] Quite apart from the devastation wrought by the Covid-19 pandemic, that is a tall order after almost

---

[105] Lazonick, "Is the Most Unproductive Firm."

[106] William Lazonick, "Innovative Enterprise or Sweatshop Economics? In Search of Foundations of Economic Analysis," *Challenge* 59, 2, 2016: 65–114 and references therein.

[107] Lazonick, "The Theory of the Market Economy"; Lazonick, "Innovative Enterprise or Sweatshop Economics?."

[108] Michael C. Jensen, "Agency Costs of Free Cash Flow, Corporate Finance, and Takeovers," *American Economic Review*, 76, 2, 1986: 323–329. Lazonick, "Is the Most Unproductive Firm," p. 22.

[109] Lazonick, "Innovative Enterprise Solves the Agency Problem."   [110] Ibid.

[111] Lazonick and O'Sullivan, "Maximizing Shareholder Value"; Lazonick, "Stock Buybacks."

[112] Biden Presidential Campaign, "Build Back Better: Joe Biden's Jobs and Economic Recovery Plan for Working Americans," Biden Harris Website, (no longer accessible).

half a century of income inequality and employment instability. The Biden administration's Build Back Better agenda includes investment in productive capabilities by two of the three types of organizations – government agencies and household units – that constitute the investment triad.

On November 15, 2021, President Biden signed into law the Infrastructure Investment and Jobs Act,[113] through which government agencies can invest in productive capabilities. Stalled in Congress is the American Families Act,[114] announced as the American Families Plan in April 2021,[115] to support household units to invest in productive capabilities. On August 9, 2022, the CHIPS and Science Act, designed primarily to support investment in semiconductor fabrication in the United States, became law.[116] On August 16, 2022, Congress passed the Inflation Reduction Act, which provides business corporations with hundreds of billions of dollars in government subsidies to confront climate change. It also enables, as of 2026, Medicaid to negotiate the prices of certain high-cost prescription drugs.[117]

Missing from the Build Back Better agenda, however, are corporate-governance reforms to ensure that the third type of organization in the investment triad – the nation's business corporations – focus on investment in productive capabilities that can generate stable and equitable growth. The very first step in a policy agenda designed to engage major US business corporations in that investment effort would be to put a halt to the trillions of dollars that they spend on stock buybacks, at the expense of rewarding the US labor force for its prior value-creating efforts and investing in the next round of innovative products that can support sustainable prosperity over the next generation. In addition to enabling the United States to confront the scourge of socioeconomic inequality, the investment triad is of fundamental importance to putting in place the productive capabilities required for both a transition to green energy and effective responses to pathogen epidemics to prevent them from becoming pandemics. Without the full participation of major US business corporations in the Build Back Better agenda, the effort at recreating a diverse, robust, upwardly mobile American middle class cannot succeed.

---

[113] US House of Representatives, "H.R. 3684 – Infrastructure Investment and Jobs Act."

[114] US House of Representatives, "H.R. 928 – American Family Act of 2021."

[115] Alana Wise, "White House Proposes $1.8 Trillion Plan for Children and Families," *NPR*, April 28, 2021, www.npr.org/2021/04/28/991357190/white-house-proposes-massive-spending-on-children-and-families.

[116] White House, "FACT SHEET: CHIPS and Science Act Will Lower Costs, Create Jobs."

[117] White House, "FACT SHEET: The Inflation Reduction Act Supports Workers and Families," *Briefing Room Press Release*, August 19, 2022, https://www.whitehouse.gov/briefing-room/statements-releases/2022/08/19/fact-sheet-the-inflation-reduction-act-supports-workers-and-families/.

When he was Vice President, Joe Biden understood that stock buybacks were undermining the productive capability of the US economy.[118] In a *Wall Street Journal* op-ed in September 2016, Biden observed: "Ever since the Securities and Exchange Commission changed the buyback rules in 1982, there has been a proliferation in share repurchases. Today buybacks are the norm." The result has been, as he put it, "a significant decline in business investment." Biden concluded his article by making a forceful statement of the need for regulation of buybacks as an integral, and important, component of government economic policy:

> The federal government can help foster private enterprise by providing worker training, building world-class infrastructure, and supporting research and innovation. But government should also take a look at regulations that promote share buybacks, tax laws that discourage long-term investment and corporate reporting standards that fail to account for long-run growth. The future of the economy depends on it.[119]

In an interview with the *Las Vegas Sun* on January 11, 2020, Biden, as a candidate for the Democratic nomination for president, criticized buybacks because they shortchange R&D investment and workers' wages. As a remedy, he said: "I'm going to reinstate (the policy) that changed under the Reagan administration, when the SEC suggested there's not a limitation on buybacks."[120] With the Covid-19 pandemic upon us, on March 20, 2020, candidate Biden tweeted:

> I am calling on every CEO in America to publicly commit now to not buying back their company's stock over the course of the next year. As workers face the physical and economic consequences of the coronavirus, our corporate leaders cannot cede responsibility for their employees.[121]

During the second quarter of 2020, buybacks by companies in the S&P 500 Index fell to about $90 billion from over $200 billion in the previous quarter. But in the second quarter of 2021, with President Biden in office, they bounced right back up to $200 billion.[122] In the third quarter of 2021, buybacks had

[118] Lazonick et al., "'Build Back Better'."

[119] Joe Biden, "How Short-Termism Saps the Economy," *Wall Street Journal*, September 27, 2016, www.wsj.com/articles/how-short-termism-saps-the-economy-1475018087.

[120] Sun Staff, "Sun's 2020 Sit-Down with Joe Biden Shines a Light on How He Will Lead the Country," *Las Vegas Sun*, January 31, 2021, https://lasvegassun.com/news/2021/jan/31/the-biden-interview-suns-2020-sit-down-with-candid/.

[121] Joe Biden, @JoeBiden, March 20, 2020, https://twitter.com/JoeBiden/status/1240998489 498288129.

[122] Edward Yardeni, Joe Abbott, and Mali Quintana, "Corporate Finance Briefing: S&P 500 Buybacks & Dividends," *Yardeni Research Inc.*, March 24, 2023. https://www.yardeni.com/pub/buybackdiv.pdf.

reached an all-time quarterly record of $235 billion, surpassing the previous peak of $220 billion in the fourth quarter of 2018,[123] when share repurchases had been fueled by the Republican tax cuts.[124] For all of 2021, at a record $882 billion, S&P 500 buybacks easily outstripped the previous annual high of $806 billion in 2018.[125]

Yet, in his first year in the White House, President Biden was virtually silent on stock buybacks.[126] In his first State of the Union Address, on March 1, 2022, there was absolutely no mention of them.[127] In the *Budget of the U.S. Government: Fiscal Year 2023*, released on March 28, 2022, the Biden administration raised the issue of buybacks in relation to stock-based executive pay.[128] But the *Budget* proposed no constraints on corporations executing buybacks. As mentioned previously, the Biden administration has said that recipients of subsidies under the CHIPS and Science Act will not be able to use the *taxpayer funds* to do buybacks or dividends, but it is not at all clear that the companies will be forbidden from doing buybacks as a condition of government financial support.

To repeat: If the leading US industrial corporations devote all their profits and more to distributions to shareholders, the Build Back Better agenda, even if enacted, cannot succeed.

The United States can start the transition from a value-extracting economy, characterized by extreme inequality, to a value-creating economy, characterized

---

[123] S&P Global, "S&P 500 buybacks Set a Record High," *PR Newswire*, December 21, 2021, https://press.spglobal.com/2021-12-21-S-P-500-Buybacks-Set-A-Record-High.

[124] Lazonick et al., "Why Stock Buybacks Are Dangerous."

[125] Bob Pisani, "Buybacks Are Poised for a Record Year, but Who Do They Help?" *CNBC*, December 30, 2021, www.cnbc.com/2021/12/30/buybacks-are-poised-for-a-record-year-but-who-do-they-help.html.

[126] For one small exception, see White House, *Building Resilient Supply Chains, Revitalizing American Manufacturing, and Fostering Broad-Based Growth*, Report, June 2021, https://www.whitehouse.gov/wp-content/uploads/2021/06/100-day-supply-chain-review-report.pdf, cites Lazonick et al., "Why Stock Buybacks Are Dangerous" on page 11, where the Executive Summary states: "A focus on maximizing short-term capital returns has led to the private sector's underinvestment in long-term resilience. For example, firms in the S&P 500 Index distributed 91 percent of net income to shareholders in either stock buybacks or dividends between 2009 and 2018. This has meant a declining share of corporate income going into R&D, new facilities or resilient production processes." But the report's Recommendations make no mention of what to do about the buybacks problem. Yet, as a highly relevant current example, Lazonick and Hopkins, "Why the CHIPS Are Down," analyzes how corporate financialization has been undermining US semiconductor fabrication.

[127] White House, "Remarks by President Biden in State of the Union Address," *Briefing Room Press Release*, March 2, 2022; see Lazonick, "Where Did You Go, Vice President Joe?," where, among other things, I suggest what President Biden could have said about stock buybacks at various points in his State of the Union address. www.whitehouse.gov/briefing-room/speeches-remarks/2022/03/02/remarks-by-president-biden-in-state-of-the-union-address/.

[128] White House, *Budget of the U.S. Government: Fiscal Year 2023*, Government Printing Office, 2022, p. 16.

by stable and equitable growth, through a five-part corporate-governance reform agenda,[129] with its intellectual rationale underpinned by the theory of innovative enterprise:

- Ban stock buybacks as open-market repurchases by rescinding SEC Rule 10b-18.
- Compensate senior executives for their contributions to value creation, and not for value extraction.
- Reconstitute corporate boards by including directors who are representatives of workers and taxpayers while excluding predatory value extractors.
- Reform the tax system so that it recognizes and supports the investment triad in enhancing productive capabilities.
- Deploy corporate profits and government taxes to launch and sustain collaborations between business corporations and government agencies that support the "collective and cumulative" careers that can enable American workers and their families to contribute to and participate in an upwardly mobile society, arming tens of millions of household units with the productive capabilities to solve the nation's existential climate, health, and security crises.

Here are brief summaries of why these reforms are needed and what changes effective policy proposals should emphasize:

Ban Stock Buybacks

The stated mission of the SEC is to "protect investors; maintain fair, orderly, and efficient markets; and facilitate capital formation."[130] By adopting and implementing Rule 10b-18, the SEC has been failing in all three components of this mission. Under Rule 10b-18, when the SEC permits massive manipulation of the stock market, it fails to protect "investors" – among whom the SEC presumably includes households as savers.

Households that allocate a portion of their savings to purchase the shares of publicly listed companies want those shares to yield an income stream from dividends (where available) while they are holding the shares, and they want to realize gains from stock-price increases when they decide to sell the shares. Only by generating innovative products can a company provide these stock

---

129 Lazonick and Shin, *Predatory Value Extraction*, Ch. 8.
130 US Securities and Exchange Commission, "About the SEC," *sec.gov*, www.sec.gov/about; US Securities and Exchange Commission, *Agency Financial Report*, fiscal year 2021, p. 4 (see also Message from the Chair Gary Gensler, p. ii). This statement of the SEC mission initially appeared in the SEC *2003 Annual Report,* p. 1, the first report issued with William H. Donaldson as SEC chair.

yields on a sustainable basis. Payment of dividends to shareholders should be determined after rewards, including wage increases, have been distributed out of profits to the company's employees – the real value creators – and after the company's needs for reinvestment of profits to remain competitive have been met. If the corporation invests in innovation and can generate higher-quality, lower-cost products, we can expect that its stock price will increase. There is no need to do stock buybacks to manipulate the company's stock price.

Stock buybacks done as open-market repurchases do not benefit households as savers, except by accident. Open-market repurchases carried out in accordance with Rule 10b-18 benefit stock-market traders – including senior corporate executives, hedge-fund managers, and Wall Street bankers – who are in the business of timing the buying and selling of shares to reap gains from stock-price changes. These traders have access to real-time information on buyback activity that households do not possess.[131] If the SEC wants to protect households that place some or all of their savings and retirement funds in outstanding corporate shares, it should rescind Rule 10b-18 and call for a ban on open-market repurchases.[132]

When the SEC permits massive manipulation of the stock market under the aegis of Rule 10b-18, it fails in its second mission: to ensure "fair, orderly, and efficient" markets. The stock market is not fair when predatory value extractors are granted the right to manipulate stock prices for their own gain, with the corporation often price gouging consumers, shortchanging suppliers, and laying off employees for the sake of increasing profits to be distributed to shareholders. The stock market is not orderly when stock prices are boosted by stock buybacks, often funded by debt as well as by profits that are increased by layoffs of workers and price-gouging of buyers.[133] In a competitive process to keep up with the market in stock-price performance, companies escalate buybacks when stock prices are high, helping to set up the manipulated stock market for a precipitous fall. By enabling manipulation of stock prices and fomenting speculation in a surging stock market, stock buybacks contribute to disorderly markets.

Moreover, there is nothing efficient about a stock market that is manipulated by stock buybacks. For households as savers, the stock market cannot be an efficient way of enhancing the value of their savings when a small number of predatory value extractors benefit from rules of the game that give insiders most

---

[131] See, for example, John Ramsay, Investors Exchange LLC, "Letter to Brent J. Fields, Securities and Exchange Commission," March 27, 2018, https://www.sec.gov/rules/petitions/2018/petn4-722.pdf.

[132] See Palladino and Lazonick, "Regulating Stock Buybacks."

[133] Lazonick et al., "Why Stock Buybacks Are Dangerous."

of the stock-market gains. If the SEC wants to use its regulatory power to make US stock markets more fair, more orderly, and more efficient, it should call for a ban on open-market repurchases rather than, as has been the case for four decades, encourage them.

Far from facilitating capital formation, as the SEC claims they do, stock buybacks undermine investment in productive capabilities, including investments in human capabilities as well as expenditures on plant and equipment. Earnings retained out of profits are the foundation of corporate finance for investment in productive capabilities, and stock buybacks, coming on top of ample dividends, have persistently depleted the retained earnings of US business corporations. Significant amounts of those distributions augment the war chests of hedge-fund activists, giving them even more power to engage in predatory value extraction.[134]

For the SEC to be positioned to use its regulatory power for the purpose of encouraging capital formation – that is, investments in productive capabilities that can generate economic growth – the US Congress should rescind Rule 10b-18. In 2018, Sen. Tammy Baldwin (D-WI) proposed precisely this reform as part of the Reward Work Act, reintroduced in the Senate by Baldwin with three cosponsors in March 2019[135] and in the House by Reps. Jésus García (D-IL), Peter DeFazio (D-OR), and Ro Khanna (D-CA) in October 2022.[136]

Redesign Executive Pay

As we have seen, executive pay in the United States is made up of several different components, of which salary and bonus are *relatively* unimportant (but by no means unsubstantial) in comparison to stock-based components, which take the form of stock options and stock awards (see Figure 2). From 1950 to 1976, stock options as a form of executive compensation were a tax dodge to enable senior corporate executives to pay the capital-gains tax rate rather than the ordinary rate (25 percent versus as high as 91 percent in the 1950s and 1960s) on a portion of their compensation.[137]

---

[134] For a detailed study, see Lazonick et al., "What We Learn about Inequality."

[135] Tammy Baldwin, "U.S. Senator Tammy Baldwin Reintroduces Legislation to Rein in Stock Buybacks and Give Workers a Voice on Corporate Boards," *Sen. Tammy Baldwin Press Release*, March 27, 2019, www.baldwin.senate.gov/news/press-releases/reward-work-act-2019.

[136] Chuy Garcia, "Representatives García, DeFazio, and Khanna Introduce Legislation Increase Worker Power and Rein in Harmful Stock Buybacks," *Rep. Chuy Garcia Press Release*, October 7, 2022, https://chuygarcia.house.gov/media/press-releases/representatives-garcia-defazio-and-khanna-reintroduce-legislation-increase-worker-power-and-rein-in-harmful-stock-buybacks.

[137] Matt Hopkins and William Lazonick, "The Mismeasure of Mammon: Uses and Abuses of Executive Pay Data," Institute for New Economic Thinking Working Paper No. 49, August 29,

In 1960, in an article in *Harvard Business Review,* "Are Stock Options Getting Out of Hand?," the dean of Harvard Law School, Erwin Griswold, criticized the tax rules on stock options for favoring a special class of people who did not make investments that justified capital gains. He argued that option grants focused the minds of executives more on speculative price movements of the company's stock than on the job of managing a large corporation.[138] Griswold's intervention provoked a vigorous public debate, from which Sen. Albert Gore (D-TN) emerged as the foremost Congressional opponent of this tax dodge.[139] Subsequent revisions in the US tax code culminated in the elimination, in the Tax Reform Act of 1976, of the capital-gains treatment for executive stock-option compensation.[140] In 1978, Graef Crystal – a compensation consultant who would later become a vocal critic of excessive executive pay – stated that qualified stock options, "once the most popular of all executive compensation devices, ... have been given the last rites by Congress."[141]

In the 1980s, however, with the personal tax rate much reduced and with the help of compensation consultants – including Crystal, who, in a *mea culpa,* exposed the executive-pay scam in his 1991 book, *In Search of Excess* – stock options as a form of compensation proliferated, not only for senior executives but also for a broad base of professional, technical, and administrative employees in the "New Economy" firms emanating from Silicon Valley.[142] In a socioeconomic process that I would call "contagious compensation," the boards of Old Economy firms began lavishing stock-based compensation on senior executives, while these companies also began to use stock options to compete with New Economy companies for personnel, including scientists, engineers, and middle managers.[143]

2016, www.ineteconomics.org/research/research-papers/the-mismeasure-of-mammon-uses-and-abuses-of-executive-pay-data.

[138] Erwin N. Griswold, "Are Stock Options Getting Out of Hand?" *Harvard Business Review,* 39, 4, 1961: 52–58.

[139] "Gore Bill Would End Stock Option Plans," *Washington Post,* April 15, 1961; Albert Gore, "How to Be Rich without Paying Taxes," *New York Times,* April 11, 1965.

[140] Hopkins and Lazonick, "The Mismeasure of Mammon," pp. 11–12.

[141] Graef Crystal, *Executive Compensation: Money, Motivation, and Imagination,* American Management Association, 1978, p. 145. See Graef S. Crystal, *In Search of Excess: The Overcompensation of the American Executive,* Norton, 1991.

[142] Lazonick, *Sustainable Prosperity.*

[143] William Lazonick, "Taking Stock: How Executive Pay Results in an Inequitable and Unstable Economy," *Franklin and Eleanor Roosevelt Institute White Paper,* June 5, 2014, https://www.theairnet.org/v3/backbone/uploads/2014/08/Lazonick_Executive_Pay_White_Paper Roosevelt_Institute.pdf; Susan Holmberg and Mark Schmitt, "The Overpaid CEO," *Democracy,* Fall 2014, https://democracyjournal.org/magazine/34/the-overpaid-ceo/; Hopkins and Lazonick, "The Mismeasure of Mammon."

Agency theorists extol the use of stock-based pay to incentivize senior executives to maximize shareholder value.[144] Yet the very existence of stock options and stock awards as components of executive pay is integral to corporate financialization. If a corporate CEO – occupying a position of strategic control that represents the pinnacle of a business career – does not have the ability to engage in innovation, no amount of stock-based compensation can induce that CEO to formulate, adopt, and implement an innovation strategy. For those who do have the requisite capabilities and are granted the opportunity to head a major company, reasonable rewards for success in investing in innovation should provide sufficient incentives to apply the work effort necessary to lead the transformation of an innovation strategy into high-quality, low-cost products.

As stock-based executive compensation is designed in the United States, it incentivizes value extraction rather than value creation. Typically, a stock option will vest over four years, with one-quarter of the shares in the option vesting at the end of each year (although many other arrangements are possible, particularly for senior executives). Provided that executives stay with their companies, they have a vast window of anywhere from six years to nine years before the options expire, during which time they can choose the particular day or days on which to exercise the options. If the executive thinks that the company's stock price will be higher in, say, six months, then, provided the option is not expiring, he or she can wait to exercise the option in accordance with that expectation.

In the case of stock awards, which unlike options do not have an exercise price that the executive must pay to obtain the shares, executives receive shares specified in the award and realize the gains when the award vests. The least complicated stock awards simply vest after a stated period of time – for example, three years from the award date if the executive is still employed by the company. More complex stock awards vest when the company hits certain "performance" metrics such as stipulated stock-price increases or earnings-per-share targets. The attainment of these financial targets may also result in additional shares being added to the award. As in the case of stock options, executives can choose to sell the shares acquired by awards to lock in the realized gains. Alternatively, they can continue to hold the shares to collect dividends and possibly reap a future stock-price gain, but any such additional income after the vesting of stock awards does not constitute compensation.

---

[144] Michael C. Jensen and Kevin J. Murphy, "Performance Pay and Top Management Incentives," *Journal of Political Economy*, 98, 2, 1990: 225–264.

The presence of a liquid stock market makes it quick and inexpensive for executives to sell the shares immediately when they exercise stock options or when they receive vested stock awards. Prior to 1991, however, under an SEC rule intended to prevent insiders from making short-swing profits, senior executives were required to hold the shares obtained from exercising an option for six months after the exercise date before realizing the gains. In May 1991, however, the SEC changed the rule so that the six-month waiting period starts when the option is *granted*, not when it is exercised. Since it always takes at least a year from the grant date for an option to vest, this change permits the senior executive to sell the acquired shares immediately upon exercising the option, locking in the realized gains.

US-style stock options, therefore, provide incentives for executives to take advantage of what they think may be short-term surges in the company's stock price. Since the timing of stock buybacks is controlled by these executives, repurchases are an ideal means for making these surges happen. Thus, by design, US-style executive stock options incentivize value extraction, not value creation. Indeed, the very way in which options are structured encourages insider trading by senior executives, especially around the execution of stock buybacks.[145] Stock awards are also often designed to elicit the same behavior, enabling senior corporate executives to enrich themselves through value extraction that comes at the expense of investment in value creation.

Even with SEC Rule 10b5-1, adopted in 2000 to give corporate executives a safe harbor against insider-trading charges in stock sales by doing them according to a pre-announced plan, top executives can time their option exercises and stock sales to increase their pay.[146] In any case, the SEC does not collect data on the dates on which stock buybacks are done, and in the four decades that Rule 10b-18 has provided a safe harbor against stock-market manipulation in doing large-scale repurchases, the SEC has not investigated any executives for trading on the material nonpublic information of the dates on which buybacks are carried out.[147]

---

[145] Robert L. Jackson, "Stock Buybacks and Corporate Cashouts," *US Securities and Exchange Commission*, June 11, 2018, www.sec.gov/news/speech/speech-jackson-061118; Lenore Palladino, "Do Corporate Insiders Use Stock Buybacks for Personal Gain?" *International Review of Applied Economics*, 34, 2, 2020: 152–174, www.tandfonline.com/doi/abs/10.1080/02692171.2019.1707787?journalCode=cira20.

[146] Allan Horwich, "The Origin, Application, Validity, and Potential Misuse of Rule 10b5-1," *The Business Lawyer*, 61, May 2007: 913–954; Alan B. Jagolinzer, "SEC Rule 10b5-1 and Insiders' Strategic Trade," *Management Science*, 55, 2, 2009: 231–259; Jesse Eisinger, "Lucky Man: Repeated Good Fortune in Timing Stock Sales," *ProPublica*, February 19, 2014, https://www.propublica.org/article/lucky-man-ceos-repeated-good-fortune-in-timing-stock-sales.

[147] Tammy Baldwin, "Letter to SEC Chair Mary Jo White," April 23, 2015, https://www.cii.org/files/Letter%20from%20Sen_%20Baldwin%20to%20SEC%20Chair%20White.pdf Mary Jo White, "Letter to Sen. Tammy Baldwin," July 13, 2015, www.documentcloud.org/documents/2272283-sec-response-to-baldwin-07132015.html#document/p1; Tammy Baldwin, "Letter to SEC Chair

In its 2023 *Budget*, President Biden takes aim at realized gains on executive pay as an incentive for senior management to do stock buybacks.

> The President also supports legislation that would align executives' interests with the long-term interests of shareholders, workers, and the economy by requiring executives to hold on to company shares that they receive for several years after receiving them, and prohibiting them from selling shares in the years after a stock buyback. This would discourage corporations from using profits to repurchase stock and enrich executives, rather than investing in long-term growth and innovation.[148]

The implementation of this proposal would be a step forward, particularly because it recognizes that buybacks undermine investment in innovation. But it does not address the immense power of hedge-fund activists as value-extracting outsiders (discussed below in the agenda to reconstitute corporate boards) in demanding that corporate executives do buybacks as a condition of retaining their positions of strategic control. For example, I do not think that Apple did $553 billion in buybacks from October 2012 through September 2022 because CEO Tim Cook wanted to inflate his pay. Apple spent a massive fortune on buybacks so that Carl Icahn and Warren Buffett, or potentially the likes of William Ackman, Daniel Loeb, Nelson Peltz, and Paul Singer, to name a few of the most prominent "value-extracting outsiders," would not use the proxy-voting system to replace Cook and his board with top management that would do their bidding in distributing the company's so-called free cash flow for the sake of MSV. Instead, in the name of MSV, Cook, Levinson, Gore, and the rest of the Apple board have done the bidding of the predatory value extractors to maintain their positions of strategic control.

If the Biden administration is intent on preventing corporate financialization from inflating executive pay, it should ask the SEC to institute the correct measurement of executives' *realized gains* on their stock-based compensation. Since 2006, in collaboration with the Financial Accounting Standards Board, the SEC has mandated, in the Summary Compensation Table (SCT) that each publicly listed company must include in its annual proxy statement (SEC Form DEF 14A), the use of estimated "fair value" (EFV) measures of executive compensation in the form of stock options and stock awards rather than the actual realized gains (ARG) that executives in fact "take home" and on which

Mary Jo White," November 16, 2015, https://www.baldwin.senate.gov/imo/media/doc/111615%20Letter%20to%20SEC.pdf; Mary Jo White, "Letter to Sen. Tammy Baldwin," January 29, 2016 (copy in the possession of the author). See also David Dayen, "SEC Admits It's Not Monitoring Stock Buybacks to Prevent Market Manipulation," *The Intercept*, August 12, 2015, https://theintercept.com/2015/08/13/sec-admits-monitoring-stock-buybacks-prevent-market-manipulation/.
[148] White House, *Budget of the U.S. Government*, p. 16.

they pay personal taxes to the Internal Revenue Service (IRS).[149] EFV measures are based on deeply flawed economics, including Black–Scholes–Merton option-pricing models for stock options, that ignore the actual drivers of stock prices: innovation, speculation, and manipulation.[150]

The estimates of the "fair value" of stock options and stock awards use grant-date prices, not the market prices of options when they are exercised and awards when they vest. Yet, it is the excess of the market price when options are exercised or awards vest over the grant-date price that incentivizes senior executives to engage in activities, including the execution of buybacks, to inflate their own pay packages. ARG measures for options and awards are not a corporate secret; each company must report these data for its CEO, CFO, and other three highest-paid executives in its annual proxy statement. It is just that the SEC requires the use of the flawed EFV measures in the SCT. As a result, not only the media but also many progressive legislators, unions, and civil-society organizations that are critical of executive pay disseminate the fictitious data on executive compensation that the SCT contains.[151]

Indeed, as Hopkins and I explain in a public comment to the SEC on the Pay Ratio Disclosure Rule,[152] under which (as required by the Dodd-Frank Act of 2010) each company reports the ratio of the pay of the CEO to that of its median employee, the calculation of this hierarchical pay disparity within the corporation is erroneous because of the use of EFV measures for CEO pay. Especially when a company's stock price is rising, actual CEO pay using ARG measures outstrips estimated CEO pay using EFV measures. For example, in 2020, as shown in Figure 2, using ARG measures of stock-based pay, the average total compensation for the 500 highest-paid US executives was $40.9 million, of which realized gains from stock awards were 38 percent and realized gains from stock options 48 percent. But using EFV measures, the average total compensation of the same 500 executives in 2020 was $16.3 million. For stock awards, average ARG was $15.5 million while EFV was $8.4 million; for stock options, average ARG was $19.5 million while average EFV was $2.0 million.

In short, in favoring EFV over ARG as the measure of stock-based pay, the SEC misinforms the public concerning the actual take-home pay of senior

---

[149] Hopkins and Lazonick, "The Mismeasure of Mammon"; William Lazonick and Matt Hopkins, "If the SEC Measured CEO Pay Packages Properly, They Would Look Even More Outrageous," *Harvard Business Review*, December 22, 2016, https://hbr.org/2016/12/if-the-sec-measured-ceo-pay-packages-properly-they-would-look-even-more-outrageous.

[150] Lazonick, "The Functions of the Stock Market."

[151] Hopkins and Lazonick, "The Mismeasure of Mammon."

[152] William Lazonick and Matt Hopkins, "Comment on the Pay Ratio Disclosure Rule," *Public Comment to the US Securities and Exchange Commission*, March 21, 2017, https://www.sec.gov/comments/pay-ratio-statement/cll3-1658300-148764.pdf.

corporate executives. Meanwhile, as is the case for all employees, these executives pay taxes on ARG to the US Treasury via their personal filings to the IRS, while the corporation that employs them correctly uses ARG in the calculation of its compensation expense in filing its corporate tax return with the IRS.

A particularly egregious example of what Hopkins and I have labeled "The Mismeasure of Mammon"[153] is the pay of John C. Martin, CEO of Gilead Sciences, in 2014 and 2015, when the pharmaceutical company was profiting immensely from the high prices of its Sovaldi/Harvoni hepatitis-C drugs. An eighteen-month Congressional inquiry by Sens. Ron Wyden (D-OR) and Charles Grassley (R-IA) probed the rationale for Gilead's pricing strategy, concluding, in a report issued on December 1, 2015, that "a key consideration in Gilead's decision-making process to determine the ultimate price of Sovaldi was setting the price such that it would not only maximize revenue, but also prepare the market for Harvoni and its even higher price."[154] But the Wyden–Grassley report makes no attempt to probe the influence and impact of Gilead's mode of executive compensation on its strategy to charge high drug prices for the sake of an exploding stock price. The objective of Gilead's executives in setting high prices was not to maximize revenue but rather to "maximize shareholder value" so that soaring stock prices would translate into enormous compensation packages.[155]

In a hard-hitting article entitled "Gilead's greed that kills," economist Jeffrey Sachs makes the case that the pricing of Sovaldi and Harvoni handed Gilead CEO Martin "the spoils of untrammeled greed":

> Gilead Sciences is an American pharmaceutical company driven by unquenchable greed. The company is causing hundreds of thousands of Americans with Hepatitis C to suffer unnecessarily and many of them to die as the result of its monopolistic practices, while public health programs face bankruptcy. Gilead CEO John C. Martin took home a reported $19 million last year in compensation – the spoils of untrammeled greed.[156]

The "reported $19 million" that Sachs cites, however, is an EFV measure of executive compensation, taken from Gilead's SCT, that vastly understates CEO

---

[153] Hopkins and Lazonick, "The Mismeasure of Mammon."

[154] Staffs of Senators Ron Wyden and Charles E. Grassley, "The Price of Sovaldi and Its Impact in the U.S. Health Care System," *US Senate, Committee on Finance*, December 1, 2015, p. 117, https://www.finance.senate.gov/ranking-members-news/wyden-grassley-sovaldi-investigation-finds-revenue-driven-pricing-strategy-behind-84-000-hepatitis-drug.

[155] Lazonick et al., "U.S. Pharma's Business Model: Why It Is Broken, and How It Can Be Fixed." See also Victor Roy and Lawrence King, "Betting on Hepatitis C: How Financial Speculation in Drug Development Influences Access to Medicines," *BMJ*, July 17, 2016, 354: i3718, https://www.bmj.com/content/354/bmj.i3718.

[156] Jeffrey Sachs, "Gilead's Greed That Kills," *Huffington Post*, July 27, 2015, https://www.huffpost.com/entry/gileads-greed-that-kills_b_7878102.

Martin's "money-in-the-bank" compensation, which includes his ARG from the exercise of stock options and the vesting of stock awards. Multiply "the spoils of untrammeled greed" by ten, and we are close to Martin's actual compensation in 2014 of $192.8 million – with 97 percent coming from realized gains of stock-based pay. In 2015, Gilead reported Martin's total annual pay in the SCT as $18.8 million. But his actual total compensation for 2015 was $232.0 million, with 98 percent from realized gains of stock-based pay.

For the twenty years of his tenure as Gilead CEO, from 1996 to 2015, Martin's reported total compensation, using EFV measures for stock-based pay, was $208.6 million; in fact, his actual take-home pay for these twenty years was $1,000.9 million, of which 13 percent was realized gains from stock options and 82 percent realized gains from stock awards.[157] Over 42 percent of Martin's $1 billion compensation accrued in 2014 and 2015. As Gilead's stock price soared in these two years. Martin realized gains on his stock-based pay at the rate of about *$20 million per month*. Buoyed by over $30 billion in net income, much of it from Sovaldi/Harvoni sales, Martin helped to boost Gilead's stock price even more by executing $15.3 billion in buybacks, thus assisting himself in further inflating his own "performance" pay.

If the preferred goal in corporate governance is to provide incentives for value creation rather than value extraction, stock-based pay for executives should be eliminated. Stock-based pay incentivizes and rewards senior executive decision-making in corporate resource allocation that foments speculation and encourages manipulation, to the detriment of innovation. Instead, senior executives should be incentivized and rewarded by metrics related to the success of the corporation in value creation. They should be compensated for investing in higher-quality products that build on their companies' distinctive productive capabilities, increasing the extent of the market to which these products are delivered, and fostering new competitive products that enhance the employment security and income of the employees upon whose skills and efforts the company relies to bring those products into existence.

More than that, senior executives should be rewarded as members of a productive organization in which there is an equitable distribution of both the gains of innovative enterprise and the costs of failure. In making resource-allocation decisions, senior executives should view profits as a precious resource that provides financial commitment necessary to support the innovation process. The use of stock buybacks should be viewed as a leading indicator of senior executives who are *not* doing their jobs and of a company that will cease to be innovative – and perhaps at some point even cease to exist.

---

[157] Lazonick et al., "U.S. Pharma's Business Model."

Reconstitute Corporate Boards

It must be emphasized that MSV is an ideology that erroneously assumes that, of all participants in the activities of the business corporation, only shareholders take the risk of whether the company will generate profits from its productive activities, and hence only shareholders have a legitimate economic claim on profits if and when they occur. Rooted in the fallacious neoclassical theory of the market economy,[158] MSV assumes that all other participants receive a market-determined, risk-free payment for productive goods and services rendered. Hence, according to this distorted view of the world, those other participants do not bear the risk of whether the company turns a profit or sustains a loss. Therefore, the MSV argument goes, shareholders, as the economy's risk-bearers, are in the best position to reallocate resources to their most efficient uses.

As a corollary, it follows from MSV ideology that only shareholders, as the economy's sole risk-takers, have a legitimate claim to be engaged directly in the exercise of corporate decision-making through representation on corporate boards of directors. In fact, in the United States, the directors of most publicly listed companies are elected by shareholders – typically by nominal ratification via proxy votes of a slate of candidates proposed by incumbent management.

The problem with this system of corporate governance, however, is that public shareholders are not the only risk-takers in the uncertain process of transforming investments in the corporation's productive capabilities into revenue-generating products. Indeed, with limited liability and access to the liquid stock market on which they can buy and sell shares at low transaction costs, public shareholders take little risk at all. If a stock price falls or a company fails to pay a dividend, public shareholders can limit their losses instantaneously by selling their shares – what has long been known as "the Wall Street walk." Moreover, public shareholders can choose to diversify their holdings across a vast array of highly liquid stocks and other financial instruments.

Since workers and taxpayers are risk-takers who invest in the firm's productive capabilities, there is a clear rationale (consistent with agency-theory logic) for extending to them the right to voting representation on corporate boards. In the US context, however, stakeholder representation on boards is viewed as a radical proposition.[159] The extension of democratic rights in corporate

---

[158] Lazonick, "The Theory of the Market Economy"; Lazonick, "Is the Most Unproductive Firm."
[159] See Susan R. Holmberg, "Fighting Short-Termism with Worker Power: Can Germany's Co-Determination System Fix American Corporate Governance?" *Roosevelt Institute*, October 2017, https://rooseveltinstitute.org/wp-content/uploads/2020/07/RI-Fighting-Short-Termism-201710.pdf;

governance to previously disenfranchised groups of people represents major social change, but radical change is urgently required given the damage that the prevailing system of US corporate governance is inflicting on the attainment of stable and equitable growth.

Shaped by the flawed ideology that public shareholding represents "ownership" of productive assets, the SEC-sanctioned proxy-voting system as it now exists undermines sustainable prosperity.[160] All board members should function as trustees who recognize the generation of innovative products as the purpose of the corporation, subject to the social norms of providing stable employment and an equitable distribution of income to the company's employees. Board members should represent the participants in the corporation – including households as workers and taxpayers – who bear the risk of value creation while those whose interest in the corporation is predatory value extraction should be excluded from directorships.

Instead, as Jang-Sup Shin and I explain in our book *Predatory Value Extraction*, over the past four decades, in the name of MSV the predatory value extractors have been able to dominate the proxy-voting process, with the looting of the business corporation via distributions to shareholders becoming the norm. From its adoption in November 1982, SEC Rule 10b-18 has given those who exercise strategic control over corporate resource allocation a license to loot the corporate treasury by means of open-market repurchases.[161] As we have also seen, stock-based executive pay gives senior corporate executives, as value-extracting insiders, an incentive to participate in this looting process. Meanwhile, powerful asset-management companies along with various pension funds and mutual funds have become value-extracting enablers as their fund managers seek to exceed quarterly yield targets by placing a portion of their funds' financial assets with the hedge funds that are the biggest corporate looters. Especially since (as discussed below) the 1996 passage of the National Securities Markets

Lenore Palladino, "Economic Democracy at Work: Why (and How) Workers Should Be Represented on US Corporate Boards," *Journal of Law and Political Economy*, 1, 3, 2021: 373–396, https://papers.ssrn.com/sol3/papers.cfm?abstract_id=3476669; William Lazonick and Ulrich Jürgens, "International Workshop Series on the German System of Codetermination," Institut für die Geschichte und Zukunft der Arbeit in collaboration with Wissenschaftszentrum-Berlin and Academic-Industry Research Network, October 2020–February 2021, https://igza.org/veranstaltung/internationaler-igza-workshop-zum-deutschen-mitbestimmungssystem/.

[160] Jang-Sup Shin, "The Subversion of Shareholder Democracy and the Rise of Hedge-Fund Activism," Institute for New Economic Thinking Working Paper No. 77, July 2018, https://www.ineteconomics.org/research/research-papers/the-subversion-of-shareholder-democracy; Lazonick and Shin, *Predatory Value Extraction*, Ch. 5.

[161] Lazonick and Jacobson, "Letter to SEC."

Improvement Act (NSMIA), these asset managers have provided both finance and proxy votes to a relatively small number of hedge-fund activists who, as value-extracting outsiders, have pushed the looting of the business corporation to new extremes.

Consider the case of GE, a once-iconic US company that in 2010–2019 was No. 14 among the largest industrial repurchasers, with $50.3 billion in buybacks (135 percent of net income) and $67.0 billion in dividends (179 percent of net income) (see Table 4).[162] On October 5, 2015, Nelson Peltz's Trian Partners made public a whitepaper, splashed with GE's logo, entitled, "Transformation Underway ... But Nobody Cares,"[163] disclosing that the hedge fund had accumulated $2.5 billion of GE's stock – its largest ever stake in a company but just about 0.9 percent of GE's outstanding shares.[164] In its whitepaper, Trian claimed that it was engaging in "constructive dialogue" with GE,[165] and that it believed that, by implementing Trian's "advice," GE could boost its stock price to $45 by 2017 – a 180 percent increase in two years. That is, Trian expected to transform its $2.5 billion stake into one worth $4.5 billion on the market plus any dividends received over the period. GE CEO Jeffrey Immelt and CFO Jeffrey Bornstein were quoted by the *Wall Street Journal* as being "completely aligned on the levers" suggested by Trian to get GE "from point A to point B." Referring to Trian's proposal to jack up GE's stock price by doing large-scale buybacks, Immelt stated: "The repurchase opportunity is right in front of us."[166]

In 2016, GE distributed $8.8 million in dividends, just a shade under 100 percent of net income, plus $22.6 billion in buybacks, 256 percent of net income. In the first quarter of 2017, however, Peltz let it be known that he wanted CEO Immelt out, and by June Immelt announced that he was stepping down.[167] In October 2017, Peltz got GE to put his son-in-law and Trian partner Edward Garden on the company's board.[168] From 2016 to 2021, GE's revenues declined from $119.7 billion to $74.2 billion, and its worldwide employment from

---

[162] The following draws on Lazonick and Hopkins, "General Electric."

[163] Trian Partners, "Transformation Underway ... But Nobody Cares," *Trian Partners Whitepaper*, October, 5, 2015, https://docplayer.net/3999887-Transformation-underway-but-nobody-cares .html.

[164] David Benoit and Ted Mann, "Activist Firm Trian Takes $2.5 Billion Stake in General Electric," *Wall Street Journal,* October 5, 2015, https://www.marketwatch.com/story/activist-firm-trian-takes-25-billion-stake-in-general-electric-2015-10-05.

[165] Trian Partners, "Transformation Underway," p. 6.

[166] Benoit and Mann, "Activist Firm Trian."

[167] Ronald Orol, "Here's How Activist Nelson Peltz Turned the Lights Out on GE CEO Jeff Immelt," *The Street,* June 12, 2017, www.thestreet.com/investing/ge-s-immelt-to-step-down-as-trian-s-peltz-hovers-14173997.

[168] Thomas Gryta, David Benoit, and Joann S. Lublin, "GE Gives Activist Trian a Seat on the Board," *Wall Street Journal*, October 9, 2017, www.wsj.com/articles/trian-takes-board-seat-at-general-electric-1507549221.

295,000 to 168,000. Over the years 2017–2021, the company losses totaled $36.8 billion. In November 2021, GE announced that it would be broken up into three companies, engaged in energy, medical equipment, and aviation – the industrial activities on which beginning in the last decades of the nineteenth century the company had been built.[169] While Peltz has sold chunks of GE stock at different points in time, the company's shares still represented about 5 percent of Trian's portfolio,[170] and Peltz and Garden pushed for the GE break up as a way of "creating" shareholder value for themselves.

To repeat, Trian Partners has never held more than 0.9 percent of GE's shares outstanding – not one cent of which, it should be added, was invested in GE's productive capabilities. So how have Peltz and son-in-law been able to exercise so much power over GE's resource-allocation decisions? What follows is a brief summary of the analysis that Shin and I lay out in chapter five of *Predatory Value Extraction*.

In 1988, the US Department of Labor issued what has become known as the "Avon letter," which deemed it a fiduciary obligation for pension funds to vote the shares in their asset portfolios. In 2003, a ruling by the SEC extended this fiduciary obligation to mutual funds,[171] thus making it much easier for a hedge-fund activist with only a small percentage of a company's shares outstanding to line up a large block of proxy votes for board elections and thus pose a credible threat to incumbent management's strategic control. In mobilizing the proxy votes, the activists can get help by lobbying the two major proxy advisory services companies, ISS and Glass Lewis, which emerged, unregulated, to dominate this specialized segment as a result of the 2003 SEC ruling, to recommend to institutional investors a slate of value-extracting candidates for election to the corporate board.[172]

Meanwhile, in the 1990s, regulatory changes had increased the tools available to hedge funds to attack incumbent corporate management, as well as the size of the "war chests" (to use Carl Icahn's term[173]) under hedge-fund management that

---

[169] Jesse Pound, "GE to Break Up into 3 Companies, Focusing on Aviation, Health Care, and Energy," *CNBC*, November 9, 2021, https://www.cnbc.com/2021/11/09/ge-to-break-up-into-3-companies-focusing-on-aviation-healthcare-and-energy.html.

[170] John Vincent, "Tracking Nelson Peltz's Trian Fund Management Portfolio – Q42021," *Seeking Alpha*, February 20, 2022, https://seekingalpha.com/article/4488678-nelson-peltzs-trian-fund-management-portfolio-q4-2021-update.

[171] US Securities and Exchange Commission, "Final Rule: Disclosure of Proxy Voting Policies and Proxy Voting Records by Registered Management Investment Companies," 17 CFR Parts 239, 249, 270, and 274; Release Nos. 33-8188, 34-47304, IC-25922; File No. S7-36-02, April 14, 2003, https://www.sec.gov/rules/2003/01/disclosure-proxy-voting-policies-and-proxy-voting-records-registered-management.

[172] Shin, "The Subversion of Shareholder Democracy": Lazonick and Shin, *Predatory Value Extraction*, Ch. 5.

[173] Lazonick et al., "What We Learn about Inequality."

finance the value-extracting attacks. In 1992 and 1999, SEC amendments to its proxy regulations enabled asset managers to communicate freely among themselves and with corporate management concerning issues of corporate control. As a result, it became much easier for hedge funds to form de facto cartels for activist campaigns.[174]

The NSMIA of 1996[175] augmented the regulatory power of the federal government, and especially the SEC, vis-à-vis the states in amending the Investment Company Act and Investment Advisers Act, both of 1940, and removed the size restrictions on hedge funds and private-equity funds that had previously been limited to ninety-nine investors to be eligible for exemption from regulation under these Acts. As a result, assets under management by unregulated hedge funds (and private-equity funds) soared from the late 1990s, augmenting the financial power of hedge-fund activists to engage in predatory value extraction while giving fund managers of pensions and university endowments, among others, stakes in activist campaigns in their quest for higher yields on their financial-security portfolios.

A reform agenda to encourage major US business corporations to participate in the investment triad would exclude predatory value extractors from director seats on corporate boards. Instead, companies should be overseen by representatives of value-creating participants in the economy, including workers and taxpayers. In addition to rescinding SEC Rule 10b-18, Sen. Tammy Baldwin's Reward Work Act would have representatives of workers as one-third of board members of each publicly listed company in the United States.[176] In August 2018, Sen. Elizabeth Warren (D-MA) introduced the Accountable Capitalism Act, which, among other things, would require US corporations with $1 billion or more in annual revenues to have worker representatives as 40 percent of board members.[177]

Reform the Corporate Tax System

Big businesses and the households that grow wealthy from their involvement in these firms must pay their fair share of taxes to reimburse the large population of

---

[174] Lazonick and Shin, *Predatory Value Extraction*, pp. 109–111. See John C. Coffee and Darius Palia, "The Wolf at the Door: The Impact of Hedge-Fund Activism on Corporate Governance," *Annals of Corporate Governance*, 1, 1, 2016: 1–94.

[175] US Congress, "National Securities Markets Improvement Act of 1996," Public Law 104–290, October 11, 1996, www.congress.gov/104/plaws/publ290/PLAW-104publ290.pdf; Paul S. Stevens and Craig S. Tyle, "Mutual Funds, Investment Advisers, and the National Securities Markets Improvement Act," *Business Lawyer (ABA)* 52, 2, 1996–1997: 419–478; David Dayen, "What Good Are Hedge Funds?" *American Prospect*, Spring 2016, https://prospect.org/power/good-hedge-funds/.

[176] Baldwin, "U.S. Senator Tammy Baldwin Reintroduces Legislation."

[177] Matthew Yglesias, "Elizabeth Warren Has a Plan to Save Capitalism," *Vox*, August 15, 2018, www.vox.com/2018/8/15/17683022/elizabeth-warren-accountable-capitalism-corporations.

households of more modest means whose tax payments have supported govern-ment investments in physical infrastructure and human capabilities. Yet MSV ideology maintains that taxes on large corporations and the wealthiest house-holds will undermine investment in the productive capabilities that can deliver more employment opportunities, higher incomes, and more rapid productivity growth. This ideology underpinned the Republican-supported Tax Cuts and Jobs Act, passed by the US Congress in December 2017.[178]

In the debate over the 2017 Act, both its advocates and critics recognized that the main corporate use of the extra income gained from lowering the corporate tax rates on domestic and repatriated profits would be increased distributions to shareholders in the form of cash dividends and stock buybacks.[179] Senate Democrats dubbed the 2017 Act #GOPTaxScam, emphasizing the use of tax breaks to fund stock buybacks.[180] As Senate Democratic Leader Chuck Schumer (D-NY) put it in a #GOPTaxScam report, issued in February 2018:

> The record-setting pace of stock buybacks is proof that companies across the country are stuffing the savings from the Republican tax bill into their own pockets and the pockets of their wealthy investors, rather than workers. These numbers prove that the bulk of the savings from this bill aren't trickling down into higher wages, but into bigger gains for giant corporations and the wealthy.[181]

As the Biden administration seeks to fund government programs to invest in both physical infrastructure and human capabilities, the recognition that the

---

[178] Tax Policy Center, "How Did the Tax Cuts and Jobs Act Change Business Taxes?" *Tax Policy Center's Briefing Book*, n.d., https://www.taxpolicycenter.org/briefing-book/how-did-tax-cuts-and-jobs-act-change-business-taxes.

[179] William Lazonick, "Congress Can Turn the Republican Tax Cuts into Middle-Class Jobs," *The Hill*, February 5, 2018, https://thehill.com/opinion/finance/372760-congress-can-turn-the-republican-tax-cuts-into-new-middle-class-jobs/; Rick Wartzman and William Lazonick, "Don't Let Pay Increases Coming Out of Tax Reform Fool You," *Washington Post*, February 6, 2018, www.washingtonpost.com/opinions/dont-let-pay-increases-coming-out-of-tax-reform-fool-you/2018/02/06/1271905a-06a6-11e8-94e8-e8b8600ade23_story.html.

[180] Senate Democrats, "SPECIAL REPORT: The #GOPTaxScam Is Setting All the Wrong Records: In Two Months, $200 Billion in Corporate Share Buybacks Have Been Announced, Overwhelmingly Funneling Huge Amounts of Money to Corporate Executives and Wealthy Shareholders While the Middle Class Gets Left Behind," *Press Release*, February 28, 2018, https://www.democrats.senate.gov/newsroom/press-releases/special-report-the-goptaxscam-is-setting-all-the-wrong-records-in-two-months-200-billion-in-corporate-share-buybacks-have-been-announced-overwhelmingly-funneling-huge-amounts-of-money-to-corporate-executives-and-wealthy-shareholders-while-the-middle-class-gets-left-behind. See Lazonick et al., "Why Stock Buybacks Are Dangerous for the Economy."

[181] Senate Democrats, "SPECIAL REPORT: The #GOPTaxScam Is Setting All the Wrong Records." See also DSCC, "#GOPTaxScam Two Years Later: 'A Lot of Stock Buybacks' for Corporate Shareholders & 'Negligible Benefits' for Workers," *Press Release*, December 17, 2019, https://www.dscc.org/news/goptaxscam-two-years-later-a-lot-of-stock-buybacks-for-corporate-shareholders-negligible-benefits-for-workers/; Lazonick et al., "Why Stock Buybacks Are Dangerous for the Economy."

prime purpose in the 2017 Act of lowering the corporate tax rate from 35 percent to 21 percent was to fund even more buybacks should make it a no-brainer that the restoration of much, if not all, of that tax cut should be integral to the Build Back Better agenda. President Biden has argued for raising the corporate tax rate to between 25 and 28 percent.[182]

If US corporations were using profits to reinvest in productive capabilities, there could be a case for a lower corporate tax rate. With growth in productive employment, a lower corporate tax rate could generate tax revenues because of the gains from innovative enterprise as well as the higher incomes and more stable employment of the labor force. The key to this supply-side scenario is corporate investment in innovation.

Recognizing rampant corporate tax avoidance, on October 28, 2021, the White House announced: "The Build Back Better framework will impose a 15 percent minimum tax on the corporate profits that large corporations – those with over $1 billion in profits – report to shareholders."[183] In the 2023 *Budget*, the Biden administration proposed to "raise the corporate tax rate to 28 percent, still well below the 35 percent rate that prevailed for most of the last several decades."[184] It would have strengthened the administration's case for lifting the corporate tax rate to observe that major US corporations had used extra profits from the 2017 tax cuts to buy back their own stock.

In September 2021, Sen. Sherrod Brown (D-OH) and Sen. Ron Wyden (D-OR) proposed that stock buybacks should be taxed at 2 percent.[185] In October, the White House's Build Back Better Framework, perhaps reflecting concern that business would view a 2-percent solution as excessive, proposed a buybacks surcharge of 1 percent.[186] There was predictable business blowback about how even a small tax on buybacks would mean the end of the stock-market boom.[187] Despite good intentions, however, whether at 2 or 1 percent, these surcharge proposals only

[182] Christina Wilkie, "Biden Open to 25% Corporate Tax Rate as Part of an Infrastructure Bill," *CNBC*, May 6, 2021, www.cnbc.com/2021/05/06/biden-says-corporate-tax-rate-should-be-between-25percent-and-28percent.html.

[183] White House, "Build Back Better Framework," *Briefing Room Press Release*, October 28, 2021, https://www.whitehouse.gov/briefing-room/statements-releases/2021/10/28/build-back-better-framework/.

[184] White House, *Budget*, p. 316.

[185] Sherrod Brown, "Brown, Wyden Unveil Major New Legislation to Tax Stock Buybacks," *Sen. Sherrod Brown Press Release*, September 10, 2021, https://www.brown.senate.gov/newsroom/press/release/brown-wyden-tax-stock-buybacks; Sabrina Eaton, "Sen. Sherrod Brown Introduces Legislation to Tax Stock Buybacks," *Cleveland.com*, September 10, 2021, https://www.cleveland.com/open/2021/09/sen-sherrod-brown-introduces-legislation-to-tax-stock-buybacks.html.

[186] White House, "Build Back Better."

[187] Eric Rosenbaum, "What a Tax on Stock Buybacks Would, and Wouldn't, Mean for the Bull Market," *CNBC*, October 8, 2021, www.cnbc.com/2021/10/08/what-a-tax-on-stock-buybacks-would-mean-for-the-bull-market.html.

serve to legitimize buybacks, and the tax revenue raised from them would come nowhere near to offsetting the immense damage to the US economy and US households that buybacks cause.[188] If the Biden administration insists on taxing rather than banning buybacks, it should set the surcharge at, say, 40 percent, with a mandatory warning banner on the corporate repurchaser's website that reads: STOCK BUYBACKS DESTROY THE MIDDLE CLASS.

As it happened, in August 2022, Democrats were forced to include the 1-percent tax on buybacks in the Inflation Reduction Act as a concession to secure the vote of Sen. Kyrsten Sinema (D-AZ) needed to pass the Act in the Senate. She declared that her vote for the Act could be had if the Democrats would drop from it a provision to put an end to capital-gains tax treatment of "carried interest" income by hedge funds, replacing it with the 1-percent buy-backs tax.[189] At a press conference held after the deal with Sinema had been struck, Senate Majority Leader Chuck Schumer (D-NY) explained:

> I believe strongly in [closing] the carried interest loophole. I have voted for it. I pushed for it, I pushed for it to be in this bill. Sen. Sinema said she would not vote for the bill, not even move to proceed, unless we took it out. So we have no choice.[190]

Still, Schumer expressed confidence that all Democrats would support the stock-buybacks tax and noted its popularity with progressive Democrats. Nevertheless, in keeping with the #GOPTaxScam campaign against the Tax Cuts and Jobs Act of 2017, Schumer took the opportunity of the Inflation Reduction Act press conference to make his position on buybacks clear:

> I hate stock buybacks. I think they are one of the most self-serving things that corporate America does. Instead of investing in workers and in training and in research and in equipment, they don't do a thing to make their company better and they artificially raise the stock price by just reducing the number of shares. They're despicable. I'd like to abolish them.

In support of Schumer's position (and presumably informing it), a growing body of research, much of it carried out by the 501(c)(3) nonprofit organization, the Academic-Industry Research Network,[191] which I head, in collaboration with the Institute for New Economic Thinking,[192] shows why, in a range of industries, stock buybacks are toxic. They are a prime cause of extreme income

[188] Lazonick et al., "Why Stock Buybacks Are Dangerous."
[189] Tobias Burns and Karl Evers-Hillstrom, "Democrats Add Stock Buyback Tax, Scrap Carried Interest to Win Sinema Over," *The Hill*, August 5, 2022, https://thehill.com/business/3590121-democrats-add-stock-buyback-tax-scrap-carried-interest-to-win-sinema-over/.
[190] Ibid.   [191] The Academic-Industry Research Network Website, https://theairnet.org/.
[192] William Lazonick Webpage, Institute for New Economic Thinking, https://www.ineteconomics.org/research/experts/wlazonick.

inequality, the disappearance of stable employment opportunity, and sagging US industrial productivity. While corporations such as Intel, Cisco, GE, and Boeing have each wasted massive sums on buybacks over the last two decades or so, the United States has lost global competitive advantage in, respectively, semiconductor fabrication, 5G and IoT, wind energy, and commercial aircraft.[193] US Big Pharma companies are among the largest stock repurchasers.[194] When Medicare starts negotiating drug prices mandated by the Inflation Reduction Act, the government should insist that the pharmaceutical companies refrain from doing buybacks so that they can use their profits to invest in drug innovation.[195]

Support Triadic Investment in Collective and Cumulative Careers

In a world of rapid technological innovation and intense global competition, the value-creating economy depends on the continuous augmentation of the productive capabilities of the labor force. That means that both higher education and the work experience of the national labor force need constant upgrading as a necessary condition for producing innovative products. Achieving productive outcomes and returning a substantial portion of the profits from the productivity gains to productive workers are fundamental to achieving sustainable prosperity.[196]

Just as companies need collective and cumulative learning to be innovative, employees need *collective and cumulative careers* (CCCs) to remain productive over working lives that now span four decades or more. Under the Old Economy business model that prevailed in the decades after World War II, companies provided CCCs through the CWOC employment norm. With the rise to dominance of the New Economy business model in the 1980s and 1990s, however, the CWOC norm disappeared.[197] New Economy start-ups could not attract talent by offering a CWOC because a CWOC was not an inducement that start-ups with uncertain futures could promise to fulfill. Rather, implementing the process

---

[193] Lazonick and Hopkins, "Why the CHIPS Are Down"; Carpenter and Lazonick, "The Pursuit of Shareholder Value"; Lazonick and Hopkins, "General Electric"; Lazonick and Sakinç, "Make Passengers Safer?."

[194] Lazonick et al., "Financialization"; William Lazonick and Öner Tulum, "Sick with 'Shareholder Value': U.S. Pharma's Financialized Business Model during the Pandemic," *Institute for New Economic Thinking*, December 6, 2022, https://www.ineteconomics.org/perspectives/blog/sick-with-shareholder-value-us-pharmas-financialized-business-model-during-the-pandemic.

[195] Rosie Collington and William Lazonick, "Pricing for Medicine Innovation: A Regulatory Approach to Support Drug Development and Patient Access," Institute for New Economic Thinking Working Paper No. 178, January 28, 2022, https://www.ineteconomics.org/research/research-papers/pricing-for-medicine-innovation-a-regulatory-approach-to-support-drug-development-and-patient-access.

[196] Lazonick et al., "'Build Back Better'." [197] Lazonick, *Sustainable Prosperity.*

that I have called "marketization," New Economy start-ups could induce talent to leave or eschew CWOC employment with Old Economy companies for the sake of stock options that could become very valuable if and when the company did an IPO on NASDAQ.[198]

This New Economy practice of using stock options to attract and retain a broad base of employees remained intact even after some start-ups became going concerns with employees in the tens of thousands. Over the course of the 1980s and 1990s, this marketization process corroded the CWOC norm at Old Economy companies, with IBM's deliberate downsizing of its labor force from 374,000 in 1990 to 220,000 in 1994 representing a pivotal case.[199] In the twenty-first century, the globalization of the labor force, particularly in advanced-technology fields, has completed the erosion of the CWOC norm in the United States, as key jobs are offshored to lower-wage areas of the world and as key employees are recruited from globalized labor supplies, often on temporary nonimmigrant visas, to fill high-end technology jobs in the United States.[200] Meanwhile, the human capabilities of older workers, accumulated through many years of education and decades of work experience, atrophy at a time when the application of those capabilities to confront new economic and social challenges is what a value-creating economy needs.

In a globalized economy with rapid technological change, the CWOC norm will not be restored. This dramatic erosion and devaluation of CWOC in the now-dominant business model has created enormous challenges for members of the US labor force to construct for themselves through interorganizational mobility the CCCs that a middle-class existence requires. CCCs have become increasingly necessary for individuals to maintain a good standard of living over an expected forty to fifty years of their working lives, with sufficient savings from employment income to sustain them for another twenty years or more in retirement. Without CCCs, people who were deemed to be highly productive in their forties may become obsolete in their fifties, or they may find that educated and experienced workers in lower-wage areas of the world have become equally or even better qualified to do their jobs.

For the sake of sustainable prosperity, social institutions must be restructured to support CCCs across business corporations and government agencies as well as civil-society organizations. There are many different paths by which individuals can structure their CCCs. Over the course of their careers, people may develop skills through a series of jobs with different employers in an interlinked network of business corporations, government agencies, and civil-society organizations. In addition, a CCC may be followed across national borders,

---

[198] Ibid.   [199] Ibid., Ch. 2.   [200] Lazonick et al., "Equality Denied."

often with employment by one multinational corporation, agency, or organization or through a more individualized search for a globalized career path.[201]

As they have been doing since the late 1980s, many of the most talented and ambitious young people embarking on careers may look for a quick hit on Wall Street or a venture-backed IPO that can provide them with enough income for a lifetime without pursuing a CCC. The problem is especially acute when the large corporations that used to be the bedrocks of CCCs support the dominance of the "financial economy" over the "productive economy" by distributing almost all, if not more, of their profits to shareholders in the form of stock buybacks and cash dividends.

In summary, how can the United States be put back on a path to stable and equitable economic growth? In my view, the policy agenda for corporate-governance reform that I have outlined is a necessary condition for sustainable prosperity: ban stock buybacks as open-market repurchases; structure executive remuneration to incentivize value creation, not value extraction; place representatives of households as workers and taxpayers on corporate boards while excluding predatory value-extractors from the exercise of strategic control; fix the broken tax system so that profitable corporations and rich households return value to the society to pay for the productive capabilities with which society supplies them, including an educated and experienced labor force; and coordinate the investment triad to enable an ever-growing proportion of the population to pursue and prosper from collective and cumulative careers.

To quote then-Vice President Joe Biden's concluding line of his September 2016 *Wall Street Journal* op-ed: "The future of the economy depends on it."

---

[201] Lazonick, *Sustainable Prosperity*, Ch. 5; Lazonick, "Labor in the Twenty-First Century."

Bibliography

Academic-Industry Research Network, https://theairnet.org.

Advanced Micro Devices, "AMD Announces $4 Billion Share Repurchase Program," *AMD Press Release*, May 19, 2021, https://d1io3yog0oux5.cloud front.net/_a1b35b0c2d1b56ad4b028627b0699c55/amd/news/2021-05-19_AMD_Announces_4_Billion_Share_Repurchase_1001.pdf.

Advanced Micro Devices, "AMD Announces New $8 Billion Share Repurchase Authorization," *AMD Press Release*, February 24, 2022, https://www.amd .com/en/press-releases/2022-02-24-amd-announces-new-8-billion-share-repurchase-authorization.

Alvaredo, F., T. Atkinson, T. Piketty, and E. Saez, "The World Top Incomes Database," *Paris School of Economics*, https://www.parisschoolofeco nomics.eu/en/news/the-top-incomes-database-new-website/.

Anon., "Gore Bill Would End Stock Option Plans," *Washington Post*, April 15, 1961.

Anon., "Crude Oil Prices – 70 Year Historical Chart," Macrotrends, https:// www.macrotrends.net/1369/crude-oil-price-history-chart.

Baldwin, Tammy, "Letter to SEC Chair Mary Jo White," April 23, 2015, https:// www.cii.org/files/Letter%20from%20Sen_%20Baldwin%20to%20SEC% 20Chair%20White.pdf.

Baldwin, Tammy, "Letter to SEC Chair Mary Jo White," November 16, 2015, https://www.baldwin.senate.gov/imo/media/doc/111615%20Letter%20to% 20SEC.pdf.

Baldwin, Tammy, "U.S. Senator Tammy Baldwin Reintroduces Legislation to Rein in Stock Buybacks and Give Workers a Voice on Corporate Boards," *Sen. Tammy Baldwin Press Release*, March 27, 2019, https://www.baldwin .senate.gov/news/press-releases/reward-work-act-2019.

Bary, Emily, "Disney Buybacks May Be in Pause until 2023, Citi Says," *MarketWatch*, April 21, 2020, https://www.marketwatch.com/story/disney-buybacks-may-be-on-pause-until-2023-citi-says-2020-04-21.

Benoit, David, and Ted Mann, "Activist Firm Trian Takes $2.5 Billion Stake in General Electric," *Wall Street Journal*, October 5, 2015, https://www.market watch.com/story/activist-firm-trian-takes-25-billion-stake-in-general-elec tric-2015-10-05.

Biden, Joe, "How Short-Termism Saps the Economy," *Wall Street Journal*, September 27, 2016, www.wsj.com/articles/how-short-termism-saps-the-economy-1475018087.

Biden, Joe, @JoeBiden, March 20, 2020, https://twitter.com/JoeBiden/status/ 1240998489498288129.

Biden Presidential Campaign, "Build Back Better: Joe Biden's Jobs and Economic Recovery Plan for Working Americans," *Biden Harris Website*, (no longer accessible).

Brown, Sherrod, "Brown, Wyden Unveil Major New Legislation to Tax Stock Buybacks," *Sen. Sherrod Brown Press Release*, September 10, 2021, https://www.brown.senate.gov/newsroom/press/release/brown-wyden-tax-stock-buybacks.

Brown, Sherrod, "Brown, Portman Urge Congressional Leadership to Revise and Swiftly Pass Legislation to Invest in Manufacturing and Address Global Semiconductor Shortage," Sherrod Brown *Press Release*, January 7, 2022, https://www.brown.senate.gov/newsroom/press/release/brown-portman-pass-manufacturing-semiconductor-shortage.

Burns, Tobias, and Karl Evers-Hillstrom, "Democrats Add Stock Buyback Tax, Scrap Carried Interest to Win Sinema over," *The Hill*, August 5, 2022, https://thehill.com/policy/finance/3590121-democrats-add-stock-buyback-tax-scrap-carried-interest-to-win-sinema-over/.

Carpenter, Marie, and William Lazonick, "The Pursuit of Shareholder Value: Cisco's Transformation from Innovation to Financialization," Institute for New Economic Thinking Working Paper No. 202, February 23, 2023, https://www.ineteconomics.org/research/research-papers/the-pursuit-of-shareholder-value-ciscos-transformation-from-innovation-to-financialization.

Chandler, Jr., Alfred D., *The Visible Hand: The Managerial Revolution in American Business*, Harvard University Press, 1977.

Chandler, Jr., Alfred D., *Scale and Scope: The Dynamics of Industrial Capitalism*, Harvard University Press, 1990.

CNBCTV18.com, , "Warren Buffett's Stake in Apple Makes over $120 Billion This Week," *CNBCTV*, January 5, 2022, *CNBC*, January 5, 2022, https://www.cnbctv18.com/business/warren-buffetts-stake-in-apple-makes-over-120-billion-this-week-12020572.htm.

CNET, "Intel CEO Pat Gelsinger! (CNET's Full Interview)," *CNET Highlights*, November 19, 2021, www.youtube.com/watch?v=_y-GWcsK6Ag&t=5s.

Coffee, John C., and Darius Palia, "The Wolf at the Door: The Impact of Hedge-Fund Activism on Corporate Governance," *Annals of Corporate Governance*, 1, 1, 2016: 1–94.

Collington, Rosie, and William Lazonick, "Pricing for Medicine Innovation: A Regulatory Approach to Support Drug Development and Patient Access," Institute for New Economic Thinking Working Paper No. 178, January 28, 2022, https://www.ineteconomics.org/research/research-papers/pricing-for-medicine-innovation-a-regulatory-approach-to-support-drug-development-and-patient-access.

Conrad, Alison M., and Kathy Cannings, "Sex Segregation in the Workplace and the Mommy Track," *Academy of Management Proceedings*, 1, 1990.

Crystal, Graef, *Executive Compensation: Money, Motivation, and Imagination*, American Management Association, 1978.

Crystal, Graef S., *In Search of Excess: The Overcompensation of the American Executive*, Norton, 1991.

Dayen, David, "SEC Admits It's Not Monitoring Stock Buybacks to Prevent Market Manipulation," *The Intercept*, August 12, 2015, https://theintercept .com/2015/08/13/sec-admits-monitoring-stock-buybacks-prevent-market-manipulation/.

Dayen, David, "What Good Are Hedge Funds?" *American Prospect*, Spring 2016, https://prospect.org/power/good-hedge-funds/.

DSCC, "#GOPTaxScam Two Years Later: 'A Lot of Stock Buybacks' for Corporate Shareholders & 'Negligible Benefits' for Workers," *Press Release*, December 17, 2019, www.dscc.org/news/goptaxscam-two-years-later-a-lot-of-stock-buybacks-for-corporate-shareholders-negligible-benefits-for-workers/.

Eaton, Sabrina, "Sen. Sherrod Brown Introduces Legislation to Tax Stock Buybacks," *Cleveland.com*, September 10, 2021, https://www.cleveland .com/open/2021/09/sen-sherrod-brown-introduces-legislation-to-tax-stock-buybacks.html.

Economic Policy Institute, "The Productivity-Pay Gap," October 2022, https:// www.epi.org/productivity-pay-gap/.

Eisinger, Jesse, "Lucky Man: Repeated Good Fortune in Timing Stock Sales," *ProPublica*, February 19, 2014, https://www.propublica.org/article/lucky-man-ceos-repeated-good-fortune-in-timing-stock-sales.

Feller, Lloyd H., and Mary Chamberlin, "Issuer Repurchases," *Review of Securities Regulation*, 17, 1, 1984: 993–998.

Feng, Kaidong, *Innovation and Industrial Development in China: A Schumpeterian Perspective on China's Economic Transformation*, Routledge, 2020.

Fortune, "Fortune 500, " *Fortune*, June 1958, July 1963, June 1968, May 1973, May 1978.

Garcia, Chuy, "Representatives García, DeFazio, and Khanna Introduce Legislation Increase Worker Power and Rein in Harmful Stock Buybacks," *Rep. Chuy Garcia Press Release*, October 7, 2022, https://chuygarcia.house .gov/media/press-releases/representatives-garcia-defazio-and-khanna-reintroduce-legislation-increase-worker-power-and-rein-in-harmful-stock-buybacks.

Gelles, David, *The Man Who Broke Capitalism: How Jack Welch Gutted the Heartland and Crushed the Soul of Corporate America—and How to Undo His Legacy*, Simon & Schuster, 2022.

Gore, Albert, "How to Be Rich without Paying Taxes," *New York Times*, April 11, 1965.

Gorman, Steve, "Gore's 'Inconvenient Truth' Wins Documentary Oscar," *Reuters*, February 25, 2007, https://www.reuters.com/article/us-oscars-gore1/goresincon venient-truth-wins-documentary-oscar-idUSN2522150720070226.

Griswold, Erwin N., "Are Stock Options Getting Out of Hand?" *Harvard Business Review*, 39, 4, 1961: 52–58.

Gryta, Thomas, and Ted Mann, *Lights Out: Pride, Delusion, and the Fall of General Electric*, HarperCollins, 2021.

Gryta, Thomas, David Benoit, and Joann S. Lublin, https://www.wsj.com/ articles/trian-takes-board-seat-at-general-electric-1507549221.

Harrison, Bennett, and Barry Bluestone, *The Great U-Turn: Corporate Restructuring and the Polarizing of America*, Basic Books, 1986.

Harrison, Bennett, Chris Tilly, and Barry Bluestone, "Wage Inequality Takes a Great U-Turn," *Challenge*, 29, 1, 1986: 26–32.

Holmberg, Susan R., "Fighting Short-Termism with Worker Power: Can Germany's Co-Determination System Fix American Corporate Governance?" *Roosevelt Institute*, October 2017, https://rooseveltinstitute .org/wp-content/uploads/2020/07/RI-Fighting-Short-Termism-201710.pdf.

Holmberg, Susan, and Mark Schmitt, "The Overpaid CEO," *Democracy*, Fall 2014, https://democracyjournal.org/magazine/34/the-overpaid-ceo/.

Hopkins, Matt, and William Lazonick, "Who Invests in the High-Tech Knowledge Base?" Institute for New Economic Thinking, Working Group on the Political Economy of Distribution Working Paper No. 14, May 2014, www.ineteconomics.org/research/research-papers/who-invests-in-the-high-tech-knowledge-base.

Hopkins, Matt, and William Lazonick, "The Mismeasure of Mammon: Uses and Abuses of Executive Pay Data," Institute for New Economic Thinking Working Paper No. 49, August 29, 2016, www.ineteconomics.org/research/ research-papers/the-mismeasure-of-mammon-uses-and-abuses-of-executive-pay-data.

Hopkins, Matt, and William Lazonick, *Executive Pay: Incentives for Innovation or Financialization?* Cambridge Elements: Corporate Governance, Cambridge University Press, forthcoming 2023.

Horwich, Allan, "The Origin, Application, Validity, and Potential Misuse of Rule 10b5-1," *The Business Lawyer*, 61, May 2007: 913–954.

Hunnicutt, Trevor, and Jonathan Stempel, "Warren Buffett Is Now Apple's Biggest Shareholder—and He Wants to Own More," *Financial Post*, May 17, 2018, https://financialpost.com/investing/rpt-wrapup-3-buffett-craves-more-apple-shares-endorses-its-buybacks.

Jackson, Robert L., "Stock Buybacks and Corporate Cashouts," *US Securities and Exchange Commission*, June 11, 2018, https://www.sec.gov/news/speech/speech-jackson-061118.

Jagolinzer, Alan B., "SEC Rule 10b5-1 and Insiders' Strategic Trade," *Management Science*, 55, 2, 2009: 231–259.

Jensen, Michael C., "Agency Costs of Free Cash Flow, Corporate Finance, and Takeovers," *American Economic Review*, 76, 2, 1986: 323–329.

Jensen, Michael C., and Kevin J. Murphy, "Performance Pay and Top Management Incentives," *Journal of Political Economy*, 98, 2, 1990: 225–264.

Krueger, Alyson, "Who Is Quiet Quitting For?" *New York Times*, August 23, 2022, www.nytimes.com/2022/08/23/style/quiet-quitting-tiktok.html.

LaPedus, Mark, "Apple Should Build a Fab," *EDN*, August 26, 2010, https://www.edn.com/apple-should-build-a-fab/.

Lazonick, William, Webpage, *Harvard Business Review*, https://hbr.org/search?term=william+lazonick.

Lazonick, William, Webpage, *Institute for New Economic Thinking*, https://www.ineteconomics.org/research/experts/wlazonick.

Lazonick, William, *Competitive Advantage on the Shop Floor*, Harvard University Press, 1990.

Lazonick, William, *Business Organization and the Myth of the Market Economy*, Cambridge University Press, 1991.

Lazonick, William, "The Theory of the Market Economy and the Social Foundations of Innovative Enterprise," *Economic and Industrial Democracy*, 24, 1, 2003: 9–44.

Lazonick, William, "Corporate Restructuring," in Stephen Ackroyd, Rose Batt, Paul Thompson, and Pamela Tolbert, eds., *The Oxford Handbook of Work and Organization*, Oxford University Press, 2004: 577–601.

Lazonick, William, "Indigenous Innovation and Economic Development: Lessons from *China's Leap into the Information Age*," *Industry & Innovation*, 11, 4, 2004: 273–298.

Lazonick, William, *Sustainable Prosperity in the New Economy? Business Organization and High-Tech Employment in the United States*, W. E. Upjohn Institute for Employment Research, 2009, https://research.upjohn.org/up_press/13/.

Lazonick, William, "The Financialization of the U.S. Corporation: What Has Been Lost, and How It Can Be Regained," *Seattle University Law Review*, 36, 2, 2013: 857–909.

Lazonick, William, "Taking Stock: How Executive Pay Results in an Inequitable and Unstable Economy," *Franklin and Eleanor Roosevelt Institute White Paper*, June 5, 2014, https://www.theairnet.org/v3/backbone/uploads/2014/08/Lazonick_Executive_Pay_White_Paper_Roosevelt_Institute.pdf.

Lazonick, William, "Profits Without Prosperity: Stock Buybacks Manipulate the Market and Leave Most Americans Worse Off," *Harvard Business Review*, September 2014: 46–55, https://hbr.org/2014/09/profits-without-prosperity.

Lazonick, William, "Numbers Show Apple Shareholders Have Already Gotten Plenty," *Harvard Business Review*, October 16, 2014, https://hbr.org/2014/10/numbers-show-apple-shareholders-have-already-gotten-plenty.

Lazonick, William, "What Apple Should Do with Its Massive Piles of Money," *Harvard Business Review*, October 20, 2014, https://hbr.org/2014/10/what-apple-should-do-with-its-massive-piles-of-money.

Lazonick, William, "Labor in the Twenty-First Century: The Top 0.1% and the Disappearing Middle Class," in Christian E. Weller, ed., *Inequality, Uncertainty, and Opportunity: The Varied and Growing Role of Finance in Labor Relations*, Cornell University Press, 2015: 143–192.

Lazonick, William, "Stock Buybacks: From Retain-and-Reinvest to Downsize-and-Distribute," *Center for Effective Public Management, Brookings Institution*, April 2015, www.brookings.edu/research/stock-buybacks-from-retain-and-reinvest-to-downsize-and-distribute/.

Lazonick, William, "Innovative Enterprise or Sweatshop Economics? In Search of Foundations of Economic Analysis," *Challenge*, 59, 2, 2016: 65–114.

Lazonick, William, "The New Normal Is 'Maximizing Shareholder Value': Predatory Value Extraction, Slowing Productivity, and the Vanishing Middle Class," *International Journal of Political Economy*, 46, 4, 2017: 217–226.

Lazonick, William, "Innovative Enterprise Solves the Agency Problem: The Theory of the Firm, Financial Flows, and Economic Performance," Institute for New Economic Thinking Working Paper No. 62, August 28, 2017, https://www.ineteconomics.org/research/research-papers/innovative-enterprise-solves-the-agency-problem.

Lazonick, William, "The Functions of the Stock Market and the Fallacies of Shareholder Value," in Ciaran Driver and Grahame Thompson, eds., *What Next for Corporate Governance?* Oxford University Press, 2018: 117–151.

Lazonick, William, "Congress Can Turn the Republican Tax Cuts into Middle-Class Jobs," *The Hill*, February 5, 2018, https://thehill.com/opinion/finance/372760-congress-can-turn-the-republican-tax-cuts-into-new-middle-class-jobs/.

Lazonick, William, "Apple's 'Capital Return' Program: Where Are the Patient Capitalists?" *Institute for New Economic Thinking*, November 13, 2018, www.ineteconomics.org/perspectives/blog/apples-capital-return-program-where-are-the-patient-capitalists.

Lazonick, William, "The Theory of Innovative Enterprise: Foundations of Economic Analysis," in Thomas Clarke, Justin O'Brien, and Charles R. T. O'Kelley, eds., *The Oxford Handbook of the Corporation*, Oxford University Press, 2019: 490–514.

Lazonick, William, "The Value-Extracting CEO: How Executive Stock-Based Pay Undermines Investment in Productive Capabilities," *Structural Change and Economic Dynamics*, 48, 2019: 53–68.

Lazonick, William, "Maximizing Shareholder Value as an Ideology of Predatory Value Extraction," in Knut Sogner and Andrea Colli, eds., *The Emergence of Corporate Governance*, Routledge, 2021: 170–186.

Lazonick, William, "The Investment Triad and Sustainable Prosperity," in Peter Creticos, Larry Bennett, Laura Owen, Costas Spirou, and Maxine Morphis-Riesbeck, eds., *The Many Futures of Work: Rethinking Expectations and Breaking Molds*, Temple University Press, 2021: 120–151.

Lazonick, William, "Is the Most Unproductive Firm the Foundation of the Most Efficient Economy? Penrosian Learning Confronts the Neoclassical Fallacy," *International Review of Applied Economics*, 36, 2, 2022: 1–32.

Lazonick, William, "Where Did You Go, Vice President Joe?" *Institute for New Economic Thinking*, March 4, 2022, https://www.ineteconomics.org/perspectives/blog/where-did-you-go-vice-president-joe.

Lazonick, William, and Matt Hopkins, "If the SEC Measured CEO Pay Packages Properly, They Would Look Even More Outrageous," *Harvard Business Review*, December 22, 2016, https://hbr.org/2016/12/if-the-sec-measured-ceo-pay-packages-properly-they-would-look-even-more-outrageous.

Lazonick, William, and Matt Hopkins, "Comment on the Pay Ratio Disclosure Rule," *Public Comment to the US Securities and Exchange Commission*, March 21, 2017, www.sec.gov/comments/pay-ratio-statement/cll3-1658300-148764.pdf.

Lazonick, William, and Matt Hopkins, "How 'Maximizing Shareholder Value' Minimized the Strategic National Stockpile," Institute for New Economic Thinking Working Paper No. 127, July 21, 2020, https://papers.ssrn.com/sol3/papers.cfm?abstract_id=3671025.

Lazonick, William, and Matt Hopkins, "General Electric in the Grip of Predatory Value Extractors," Academic-Industry Research Network unpublished note, April 4, 2021, as a contribution to Nick Juravich and Arthur C. Wheaton, "Building a Sustainable Future for General Electric in Schenectady, New York, and Lynn, Massachusetts," School of Industrial and Labor Relations, Cornell University, and Labor Resource Center, UMass Boston, November 2021, https://www.umb.edu/media/umassbos ton/content-assets/lili-boulanger/pdf/UMB.Cornell.GE.Report.pdf.

Lazonick, William, and Matt Hopkins, "How Intel Financialized and Lost Leadership in Semiconductor Fabrication," *Institute for New Economic Thinking*, July 7, 2021, www.ineteconomics.org/perspectives/blog/how-intel-financialized-and-lost-leadership-in-semiconductor-fabrication.

Lazonick, William, and Matt Hopkins, "Why the CHIPS Are Down: Stock Buybacks and Subsidies in the U.S. Semiconductor Industry," Institute for New Economic Thinking Working Paper No. 165, November 1, 2021, https://www.ineteconomics.org/research/research-papers/why-the-chips-are-down-stock-buybacks-and-subsidies-in-the-u-s-semiconductor-industry.

Lazonick, William, and Ken Jacobson, "Letter to SEC: How Stock Buybacks Undermine Investment in Innovation for the Sake of Stock-Price Manipulation," *Institute for New Economic Thinking*, April 1, 2022, https://www.ineteconomics.org/perspectives/blog/letter-to-sec-a-policy-frame work-for-attaining-sustainable-prosperity-in-the-united-states.

Lazonick, William, and Ulrich Jürgens, "International Workshop Series on the German System of Codetermination," Institut für die Geschichte und Zukunft der Arbeit in collaboration with Wissenschaftszentrum-Berlin and Academic-Industry Research Network, October 2020–February 2021, https://igza.org/veranstaltung/internationaler-igza-workshop-zum-deutschen-mitbestimmungs system/.

Lazonick, William, and Mariana Mazzucato, "The Risk-Reward Nexus in the Innovation-Inequality Relationship," *Industrial and Corporate Change*, 22, 4, 2013: 1093–1128.

Lazonick, William, and Mary O'Sullivan, "Maximizing Shareholder Value: A New Ideology for Corporate Governance," *Economy and Society*, 29, 1, 2000: 13–35.

Lazonick, William, and Mary O'Sullivan, eds., *Corporate Governance and Sustainable Prosperity*, Palgrave, 2002.

Lazonick, William, and Mustafa Erdem Sakinç, "Make Passengers Safer? Boeing Just Made Shareholders Richer," *American Prospect*, May 31, 2019, https://prospect.org/environment/make-passengers-safer-boeing-just-made-shareholders-richer./.

Lazonick, William, and Jang-Sup Shin, *Predatory Value Extraction: How the Looting of the Business Corporation Became the US Norm and How Sustainable Prosperity Can Be Restored*, Oxford University Press, 2020.

Lazonick, William, and Öner Tulum, "Sick with 'Shareholder Value': U.S. Pharma's Financialized Business Model during the Pandemic," *Institute for New Economic Thinking*, December 6, 2022, https://www.ineteconomics .org/perspectives/blog/sick-with-shareholder-value-us-pharmas-financia lized-business-model-during-the-pandemic.

Lazonick, William, and Öner Tulum, "US Biopharmaceutical Finance and the Sustainability of the Biotech Business Model," *Research Policy*, 40, 9, 2011: 1170–1187.

Lazonick, William, Matt Hopkins, and Ken Jacobson, "What We Learn about Inequality from Carl Icahn's $2 Billion 'No Brainer'," *Institute for New Economic Thinking*, June 6, 2016, https://www.ineteconomics.org/perspec tives/blog/what-we-learn-about-inequality-from-carl-icahns-2-billion-apple-no-brainer.

Lazonick, William, Mariana Mazzucato, and Öner Tulum, "Apple's Changing Business Model: What Should the World's Richest Company Do With All Those Profits?" *Accounting Forum*, 37, 4, 2013: 249–267.

Lazonick, William, Philip Moss, and Joshua Weitz, "The Equal Employment Opportunity Omission," Institute for New Economic Thinking Working Paper No. 53, December 5, 2016, https://www.ineteconomics.org/research/ research-papers/the-equal-employment-opportunity-omission.

Lazonick, William, Philip Moss, and Joshua Weitz, "How the Disappearance of Unionized Jobs Obliterated an Emergent Black Middle Class," Institute for New Economic Thinking Working Paper No. 125, June 15, 2020, https:// www.ineteconomics.org/research/research-papers/how-the-disappearance-of-unionized-jobs-obliterated-an-emergent-black-middle-class.

Lazonick, William, Philip Moss, and Joshua Weitz, "'Build Back Better' Needs an Agenda for Upward Mobility," *Institute for New Economic Thinking*, January 25, 2021, https://www.ineteconomics.org/perspectives/blog/build-back-better-needs-an-agenda-for-upward-mobility.

Lazonick, William, Philip Moss, and Joshua Weitz, "The Unmaking of the Black Blue-Collar Middle Class," Institute for New Economic Thinking Working Paper No. 159, May 20, 2021, https://www.ineteconomics.org/ research/research-papers/the-unmaking-of-the-black-blue-collar-middle-class.

Lazonick, William, Philip Moss, and Joshua Weitz, "Equality Denied: Tech and African Americans," Institute for New Economic Thinking Working Paper

No. 177, February 18, 2022, www.ineteconomics.org/research/research-papers/equality-denied-tech-and-african-americans.

Lazonick, William, Mustafa Erdem Sakinç, and Matt Hopkins "Why Stock Buybacks Are Dangerous for the Economy," *Harvard Business Review*, January 7, 2020, https://hbr.org/2020/01/why-stock-buybacks-are-danger ous-for-the-economy?ab=hero-subleft-.

Lazonick, William, Philip Moss, Hal Salzman, and Öner Tulum "Skill Development and Sustainable Prosperity: Collective and Cumulative Careers versus Skill-Biased Technical Change," Institute for New Economic Thinking Working Group on the Political Economy of Distribution Working Paper No. 7, December 2014, https://www.ineteco nomics.org/research/research-papers/skill-development-and-sustainable-prosperity-cumulative-and-collective-careers-versus-skill-biased-technical-change.

Lazonick, William, Öner Tulum, Matt Hopkins, Mustafa Erdem Sakinç, and Ken Jacobson, "Financialization of the U.S. Pharmaceutical Industry," *Institute for New Economic Thinking*, December 2, 2019, https://www .ineteconomics.org/perspectives/blog/financialization-us-pharma-industry.

Leonhardt, David, "Our Broken Economy, in One Simple Chart," *New York Times*, August 7, 2017, https://www.nytimes.com/interactive/2017/08/07/ opinion/leonhardt-income-inequality.html.

Li, Yin, and William Lazonick, "China's Development Path: Government, Business, and Globalization in an Innovating Economy," Institute for New Economic Thinking Working Paper No. 190, August 11, 2022, https://www .ineteconomics.org/research/research-papers/chinas-development-path-gov ernment-business-and-globalization-in-an-innovating-economy.

Lu, Qiwen, *China's Leap into the Information Age: Innovation and Organization in the Computer industry*, Oxford University Press, 2000.

Mishel, Lawrence, and Josh Bivens, "Identifying the Policy Levers Generating Wage Suppression and Wage Inequality," *Economic Policy Institute Report*, May 13, 2021, https://www.epi.org/unequalpower/publications/wage-sup pression-inequality/.

National Institutes of Health, Office of Budget, "Appropriations History by Institute/Center (1938 to Present)," https://officeofbudget.od.nih.gov/ approp_hist.html.

National Institutes of Health, Office of Budget, "Supplementary Appropriation Data Table for History of Congressional Appropriations, *Fiscal Years 2020–2022*," https://officeofbudget.od.nih.gov/pdfs/FY22/Approp%20History% 20by%20IC%20FY%202020%20-%20FY%202022.pdf.

Northrup, Herbert R., and Richard L. Rowan, *The Negro and Employment Opportunity: Problems and Practices*, The University of Michigan, 1965.

Orol, Ronald, "Here's How Activist Nelson Peltz Turned the Lights Out on GE CEO Jeff Immelt," *The Street*, June 12, 2017, https://www.thestreet.com/investing/ge-s-immelt-to-step-down-as-trian-s-peltz-hovers-14173997.

O'Sullivan, Mary A., *Contests for Corporate Control: Corporate Governance and Economic Performance in the United States and Germany*, Oxford University Press, 2000.

Palladino, Lenore, "The $1 Trillion Question: New Approaches to Regulating Stock Buybacks," *Yale Journal of Regulation*, 36, 2018: 89–105, https://papers.ssrn.com/sol3/papers.cfm?abstract_id=3274357.

Palladino, Lenore, "Do Corporate Insiders Use Stock Buybacks for Personal Gain?" *International Review of Applied Economics*, 34, 2, 2020: 152–174, www.tandfonline.com/doi/abs/10.1080/02692171.2019.1707787?journalCode=cira20.

Palladino, Lenore, "Economic Democracy at Work: Why (and How) Workers Should Be Represented on US Corporate Boards," *Journal of Law and Political Economy*, 1, 3, 2021: 373–396, https://papers.ssrn.com/sol3/papers.cfm?abstract_id=3476669.

Palladino, Lenore, and William Lazonick, "Regulating Stock Buybacks: The $6.3 Trillion Question," *International Review of Applied Economics*, September 26, 2022, www.tandfonline.com/doi/full/10.1080/02692171.2022.2123459.

Pfizer Inc., "Event Brief of Q4 2019 Pfizer Inc Earnings Call – Final," *CQ FD Disclosure*, January 28, 2020.

Pfizer Inc., "Pfizer Reports First-Quarter 2022 Results," *Pfizer Press Release*, May 3, 2022. https://s28.q4cdn.com/781576035/files/doc_financials/2022/q1/Q1-2022-PFE-Earnings-Release.pdf.

Pfizer Inc., "Pfizer's Second Quarter Sees Historical Sales and Bold Goals," *Pfizer Investor Insights*, July 28, 2022, https://insights.pfizer.com/second-quarter-results/.

Pisani, Bob, "Buybacks Are Poised for a Record Year, but Who Do They Help?" *CNBC*, December 30, 2021, www.cnbc.com/2021/12/30/buybacks-are-poised-for-a-record-year-but-who-do-they-help.html.

Pound, Jesse, "GE to Break Up into 3 Companies, Focusing on Aviation, Health Care, and Energy," *CNBC*, November 9, 2021, https://www.cnbc.com/2021/11/09/ge-to-break-up-into-3-companies-focusing-on-aviation-healthcare-and-energy.html.

Ramsay, John, Investors Exchange LLC, "Letter to Brent J. Fields, Securities and Exchange Commission," March 27, 2018, https://www.sec.gov/rules/petitions/2018/petn4-722.pdf.

Robison, Peter, *Flying Blind: The 737 MAX Tragedy and the Fall of Boeing*, Knopf Doubleday, 2021.

Rosalsky, Greg, and Alina Selyukh, "The Economics behind 'Quiet Quitting'—and What We Should Call It Instead," *NPR*, September 13, 2022, https://www.npr.org/sections/money/2022/09/13/1122059402/the-economics-behind-quiet-quitting-and-what-we-should-call-it-instead.

Rosenbaum, Eric, "What a Tax on Stock Buybacks Would, and Wouldn't, Mean for the Bull Market," *CNBC*, October 8, 2021, https://www.cnbc.com/2021/10/08/what-a-tax-on-stock-buybacks-would-mean-for-the-bull-market.html.

Roy, Victor, and Lawrence King, "Betting on Hepatitis C: How Financial Speculation in Drug Development Influences Access to Medicines," *BMJ*, July 17, 20116, 354: i3718, www.bmj.com/content/354/bmj.i3718.

S&P Global, "S&P 500 Buybacks Set a Record High," *PR Newswire*, December 21, 2021, https://press.spglobal.com/2021-12-21-S-P-500-Buybacks-Set-A-Record-High.

Sachs, Jeffrey, "Gilead's Greed That Kills," *Huffington Post*, July 27, 2015, www.huffpost.com/entry/gileads-greed-that-kills_b_7878102.

Semiconductor Industry Association "SIA calls for House passage of legislation to advance U.S. technology leadership," *SIA*, June 28, 2021, https://www.semiconductors.org/sia-calls-for-house-passage-of-legislation-to-advance-u-s-technology-leadership/.

Semiconductor Industry Association, 'SIA Members: Working together to advance the U.S. semiconductor industry,' SIA, https://www.semiconductors.org/about/members/.

Semiconductors in America Coalition, "Letter: SIAC calls on congressional leaders to fund CHIPS Act ," SIAC, July 28, 2021, www.chipsinamerica.org.

Senate Democrats, "SPECIAL REPORT: The #GOPTaxScam Is Setting All The Wrong Records: In Two Months, $200 Billion in Corporate Share Buybacks Have Been Announced, Overwhelmingly Funneling Huge Amounts of Money to Corporate Executives and Wealthy Shareholders While the Middle Class Gets Left Behind," *Press Release*, February 28, 2018, https://www.democrats.senate.gov/newsroom/press-releases/special-report-the-goptaxscam-is-setting-all-the-wrong-records-in-two-months-200-billion-in-corporate-share-buybacks-have-been-announced-overwhelmingly-funneling-huge-amounts-of-money-to-corporate-executives-and-wealthy-shareholders-while-the-middle-class-gets-left-behind.

Sencer, David J. "CDC Museum COVID-19 Timeline," *Centers for Disease Control and Prevention*, www.cdc.gov/museum/timeline/covid19.html.

Shilov, Anton, "Texas to Get Multiple New Fabs as Samsung and TI to Spend $47 Billion on New Facilities," *AnandTech*, November 24, 2021, https://www.anandtech.com/show/17086/texas-to-get-multiple-new-fabs-as-samsung-and-ti-to-spend-47-billion-on-new-facilities.

Shin, Jang-Sup, "The Subversion of Shareholder Democracy and the Rise of Hedge-Fund Activism," Institute for New Economic Thinking Working Paper No. 77, July 2018, https://www.ineteconomics.org/research/research-papers/the-subversion-of-shareholder-democracy.

Staffs of Senators Ron Wyden and Charles E. Grassley, "The Price of Sovaldi and Its Impact in the U.S. Health Care System," *US Senate, Committee on Finance*, December 1, 2015ff, www.finance.senate.gov/ranking-members-news/wyden-grassley-sovaldi-investigation-finds-revenue-driven-pricing-strategy-behind-84-000-hepatitis-drug.

Stahl, Lesley, "Chip Shortage Highlights U.S. Dependence on Fragile Supply Chain," *60 Minutes*, May 2, 2021, www.cbsnews.com/news/semiconductor-chip-shortage-60-minutes-2021-05-02/.

Standard and Poor's, "S&P Compustat Database."

Stevens, Paul S., and Craig S. Tyle, "Mutual Funds, Investment Advisers, and the National Securities Markets Improvement Act," *Business Lawyer (ABA)*, 52, 2, 1996–1997: 419–478.

Sun Staff, "Sun's 2020 Sit-Down with Joe Biden Shines a Light on How He Will Lead the Country," *Las Vegas Sun*, January 31, 2021, https://lasvegassun.com/news/2021/jan/31/the-biden-interview-suns-2020-sit-down-with-candid/.

Swanson, Ana, "Biden Administration Releases Plan for $50 Billion Investment in Chips," *New York Times*, September 6, 2022, https://www.nytimes.com/2022/09/06/business/economy/biden-tech-chips.html/.

Tarasov, Katie, "Inside TSMC, the Taiwanese Chipmaking Giant That's Building a New Plant in Phoenix," CNBC, October 16, 2021, https://www.cnbc.com/2021/10/16/tsmc-taiwanese-chipmaker-ramping-production-to-end-chip-shortage.html.

Tax Policy Center, "How Did the Tax Cuts and Jobs Act Change Business Taxes?" *Tax Policy Center's Briefing Book*, n.d., https://www.taxpolicycenter.org/briefing-book/how-did-tax-cuts-and-jobs-act-change-business-taxes.

The Academic-Industry Research Network Website, https://theairnet.org/.

Trian Partners, "Transformation Underway … But Nobody Cares," *Trian Partners Whitepaper*, October, 5, 2015, https://docplayer.net/3999887-Transformation-underway-but-nobody-cares.html.

Tulum, Öner, and William Lazonick, "Financialized Corporations in a National Innovation System: The US Pharmaceutical Industry," *International Journal of Political Economy*, 47, 3–4, 2018: 281–316.

Tulum, Öner, Antonio Andreoni, and William Lazonick, *From Financialisation to Innovation in UK* Big Pharma: *AstraZeneca and GlaxoSmithKline*, Cambridge Elements: Reinventing Capitalism, Cambridge University Press, 2022, www.cambridge.org/core/elements/from-financialisation-to-innovation-in-uk-big-pharma/A077D6158F0A945ED53F3F125EE0650F.

US Census Bureau, "2019 SUSB Annual Data Tables by Establishment Industry," *Data and Maps*, February 2022, https://www.census.gov/data/tables/2019/econ/susb/2019-susb-annual.html.

US Census Bureau, "Income Gini Ratio of Families by Race of Householder, All Races [GINIALLRF]," *FRED, Federal Reserve Bank of St. Louis*, September 21, 2022, https://fred.stlouisfed.org/series/GINIALLRF.

US Congress, "National Securities Markets Improvement Act of 1996," *Public Law 104–290*, October 11, 1996, https://www.congress.gov/104/plaws/publ290/PLAW-104publ290.pdf.

US Department of Commerce, "Commerce Department Launches CHIPS.gov for CHIPS Program," *DOC Press Release*, August 25, 2022, https://www.commerce.gov/news/press-releases/2022/08/commerce-department-launches-chipsgov-chips-program-implementation.

US House of Representatives, "H.R. 928 – American Family Act of 2021," 117th Congress (2021–2022), *Congress.gov*, February 8, 2021, https://www.congress.gov/bill/117th-congress/house-bill/928.

US House of Representatives, "H.R. 3684 – Infrastructure Investment and Jobs Act," 117th Congress (2021–2022), *Congress.gov*, November 15, 2021, www.congress.gov/bill/117th-congress/house-bill/3684/text.

US House of Representatives, "H.R. 4346 – Chips and Sciences Act," 117th Congress (2021–2022), *Congress.gov*, August 9, 2022, https://www.congress.gov/bill/117th-congress/house-bill/4346.

US House of Representatives, "H.R. 5376 – Inflation Reduction Act of 2022," 117th Congress (2021–2022), *Congress.gov*, August 16, 2022, https://www.congress.gov/bill/117th-congress/house-bill/5376/text.

US Securities and Exchange Commission, "About the SEC," *sec.gov*, https://www.sec.gov/about.

US Securities and Exchange Commission, "Division of Trading and Markets: Answers to Frequently Asked Questions Concerning Rule 10b-18 ('Safe Harbor' for Issuer Repurchases)," *SEC Division of Trading and Markets*, www.sec.gov/divisions/marketreg/r10b18faq0504.htm.

US Securities and Exchange Commission, "Purchases of Certain Equity Securities by the Issuer and Others; Adoption of Safe Harbor," November 17, 1982, *Federal Register* 47, 228, November 26, 1982: 53333–53341.

US Securities and Exchange Commission, "Final Rule: Disclosure of Proxy Voting Policies and Proxy Voting Records by Registered Management Investment Companies," 17 CFR Parts 239, 249, 270, and 274; Release Nos. 33-8188, 34-47304, IC-25922; File No. S7-36-02, April 14, 2003, https://www.sec.gov/rules/2003/01/disclosure-proxy-voting-policies-and-proxy-voting-records-registered-management.

US Securities and Exchange Commission, *Agency Financial Report*, fiscal year 2021.

Vincent, John, "Tracking Nelson Peltz's Trian Fund Management Portfolio – Q42021," *Seeking Alpha*, February 20, 2022, https://seekingalpha.com/article/4488678-nelson-peltzs-trian-fund-management-portfolio-q4-2021-update.

Warren, Sen. Elizabeth, and Sen. Tammy Baldwin and Reps. Sean Casten, Jamaal Bowman, Pramila Jayapal, and Bill Foster, "Letter to Commerce Secretary Gina Raimondo," October 4, 2022, https://www.warren.senate.gov/imo/media/doc/2022.10.04%20Letter%20to%20Commerce%20re%20CHIPS%20Stock%20Buybacks.pdf.

Wartzman, Rick, and William Lazonick, "Don't Let Pay Increases Coming Out of Tax Reform Fool You," *Washington Post*, February 6, 2018, https://www.washingtonpost.com/opinions/dont-let-pay-increases-coming-out-of-tax-reform-fool-you/2018/02/06/1271905a-06a6-11e8-94e8-e8b8600ade23_story.html.

Weber, Jonathan, "Is Pfizer Stock a Buy after Strong Earnings? Massive Profits Won't Last," *Seeking Alpha*, August 4, 2022, https://seekingalpha.com/article/4529640-is-pfizer-stock-buy-after-strong-earnings.

Weitz, Joshua, William Lazonick, and Philip Moss, "Employment Mobility and the Belated Emergence of the Black Middle Class," Institute for New Economic Thinking Working Paper No. 143, January 2, 2021, https://www.ineteconomics.org/research/research-papers/employment-mobility-and-the-belated-emergence-of-the-black-middle-class.

White House, *Building Resilient Supply Chains, Revitalizing American Manufacturing, and Fostering Broad-Based Growth*, Report, June 2021, www.whitehouse.gov/wp-content/uploads/2021/06/100-day-supply-chain-review-report.pdf.

White House, "Build Back Better Framework," *Briefing Room Press Release*, October 28, 2021, https://www.whitehouse.gov/briefing-room/statements-releases/2021/10/28/build-back-better-framework/.

White House, *Budget of the U.S. Government: Fiscal Year 2023*, Government Printing Office, 2022.

White House, "Remarks by President Biden in State of the Union Address," *Briefing Room Press Release*, March 2, 2022, https://www.whitehouse.gov/briefing-room/speeches-remarks/2022/03/02/remarks-by-president-biden-in-state-of-the-union-address/.

White House, "FACT SHEET: CHIPS and Science Act Will Lower Costs, Create Jobs, Strengthen Supply Chains, and Counter China," *Briefing Room Press Release*, August 9, 2022, https://www.whitehouse.gov/briefing-room/statements-releases/2022/08/09/fact-sheet-chips-and-science-act-will-lower-costs-create-jobs-strengthen-supply-chains-and-counter-china/.

White House, "FACT SHEET: The Inflation Reduction Act Supports Workers and Families," *Briefing Room Press Release*, August 19, 2022, https://www.whitehouse.gov/briefing-room/statements-releases/2022/08/19/fact-sheet-the-inflation-reduction-act-supports-workers-and-families/.

White, Mary Jo, "Letter to Sen. Tammy Baldwin," July 13, 2015, https://www.documentcloud.org/documents/2272283-sec-58.

White, Mary Jo, "Letter to Sen. Tammy Baldwin," January 29, 2016 (copy in the possession of the author).

Wikipedia, "Arthur D. Levinson," *Wikipedia*, https://en.wikipedia.org/wiki/Arthur_D._Levinson.

Wilkie, Christina, "Biden Open to 25% Corporate Tax Rate as Part of an Infrastructure Bill," *CNBC*, May 6, 2021, https://www.cnbc.com/2021/05/06/biden-says-corporate-tax-rate-should-be-between-25percent-and-28percent.html.

Wise, Alana, "White House Proposes $1.8 Trillion Plan for Children and Families," *NPR*, April 28, 2021, www.npr.org/2021/04/28/991357190/white-house-proposes-massive-spending-on-children-and-families.

WRAL TechWire, "Apple CEO Confirms Commitment to Build New Campus, Hire 20,000 New Employees," *WRAL*, June 15, 2018, https://wraltechwire.com/2018/06/15/apple-ceo-reaffirms-commitment-to-build-new-campus-hire-20000-new-employees/.

Yahoo Finance, "Historical Stock Prices," https://finance.yahoo.com/.

Yardeni, Edward, Joe Abbott, and Mali Quintana, "Corporate Finance Briefing: S&P 500 Buybacks & Dividends," *Yardeni Research Inc.*, March 24, 2023, www.yardeni.com/pub/buybackdiv.pdf.

Yglesias, Matthew, "Elizabeth Warren Has a Plan to Save Capitalism," *Vox*, August 15, 2018, www.vox.com/2018/8/15/17683022/elizabeth-warren-accountable-capitalism-corporations.

Zhou, Yu, William Lazonick, and Yifei Sun, eds., *China as an Innovation Nation*, Oxford University Press, 2016.

Acknowledgments

This Cambridge Element updates and expands William Lazonick, "Investing in Innovation: A Policy Framework for Attaining Sustainable Prosperity in the United States," Institute for New Economic Thinking Working Paper No. 182, March 30, 2022. The analysis that I put forth in this Element owes much to discussions with Marie Carpenter, Matt Hopkins, Ken Jacobson, Les Leopold, Lenore Palladino, Mustafa Erdem Sakinç, Jang-Sup Shin, and Öner Tulum of the Academic-Industry Research Network, and Tom Ferguson of the Institute for New Economic Thinking (INET). I am grateful for research funding from INET as well as fellowships from the Open Society Foundations and the Canadian Institute for Advanced Research Program on Innovation, Equity & the Future of Prosperity in support of this work.

Dedication

In memory of François Chesnais (1934–2022).

Cambridge Elements ≡

Corporate Governance

Thomas Clarke

UTS Business School, University of Technology Sydney

Thomas Clarke is Professor of Corporate Governance at the UTS Business School of the University of Technology Sydney. His work focuses on the institutional diversity of corporate governance and his most recent book is *International Corporate Governance* (Second Edition 2017). He is interested in questions about the purposes of the corporation, and the convergence of the concerns of corporate governance and corporate sustainability.

About the Series

The series Elements in Corporate Governance focuses on the significant emerging field of corporate governance. Authoritative, lively and compelling analyses include expert surveys of the foundations of the discipline, original insights into controversial debates, frontier developments, and masterclasses on key issues. Its areas of interest include empirical studies of corporate governance in practice, regional institutional diversity, emerging fields, key problems and core theoretical perspectives.

Cambridge Elements ☰

Corporate Governance

Printed in the USA
CPSIA information can be obtained
at www.ICGtesting.com
LVHW011300150324
774517LV00048B/2549